HEAR MY CONFESSION

HEAR MY CONFESSION

Father Joseph Orsini

Logos International
Plainfield, New Jersey

Scripture quotations are taken from the
Revised Standard Version of the Bible
unless otherwise indicated. Used by permission.

Published by Logos International
Plainfield, New Jersey 07061

To my mother

Contents

HEAR MY CONFESSION

Early Years

I was the last of seven children. We were of Italian immigrant background living in a neighborhood of varied ethnic groups, mostly Roman Catholic. The strongest influence in my life, at least for the first six years, was my dear papa, Giuseppe, after whom I was named. My memory pictures him as a loving yet firm man whose gentleness, compassion and warmth had won the admiration of family and friends. I was the apple of his eye, his baby boy. I can remember many special times, such as when he would take me to a playground, buy me ice cream, or allow me to help when the family gathered around the kitchen table to make delicious Italian cookies. He was my protector, especially when my childish antics—as often happened—exasperated my mama. Whenever mama wanted to discipline me, papa would intervene and say "Carmela, he's only a baby, he didn't mean it." Snuggled in his arms, I would peek out at her from the safety of his strong hands, and invariably mama would soften and begin to smile. I then would run to her outstretched arms and cover her face with my tiny kisses and all would be right with the world again.

Since I was the youngest and the family was large, it was my privilege to sleep in mama and papa's large brass bed. That bed became an altar where I first learned my prayers and heard the wonderful stories about Jesus and the saints, especially on long cold winter nights, warmed by my parents' love and cloth-wrapped bricks which had been heated on the kitchen stove. We were not rich by the world's standards, but the love and intimacy we shared made me a little king. Early every morning I would awaken to see papa arise, wash, dress, put a pot of coffee on the stove, and leave to walk the few blocks to attend Mass. I often heard mama say that he was *"troppo cattolico"* which meant that he took his religion seriously. Papa would not think of going to work without asking God's blessing upon himself and his family by attending daily Mass first. When he returned we would have a simple breakfast of coffee laced with hot milk and sugar made into a sort of porridge by the addition of chunks of toasted Italian bread. Afterwards, all of the children at home, my brothers Dominick, Anthony, Oreste and my sister Evelyn (my brother Leo was married and lived close by, but my other brother, John, also married, was a soldier away in Europe during World War II) would line up to kiss papa goodbye and to say *"sa benedica papa"* (God bless you, papa) before he left for work and all of us children for school.

On the morning of November 17, 1943, we went through the same ritual, except that mama said: "Beppe [Joe], don't go to work today. Stay home. I have an awful feeling that something bad is going to happen today."

Papa smiled his easy smile, kissed her and replied, "Don't worry, nothing's going to happen," and off he went. Mama kept me home from school that day because she felt that something was wrong. Early that afternoon someone knocked on our door. Mama opened the door to a police officer.

"Mrs. Orsini?"

"Yes???"

"Mrs. Orsini, your husband was in an accident at work."

Mama intuitively knew the truth. Papa was dead. What happened after that was a whirlwind of confusing and numbing sadness. I was only six years old, but I knew my papa would never return to our house. My heart was broken. Yet, in my innocence, I hoped that he would.

It was only later in my life that I discovered the details of my father's death. He worked on the old Pennsylvania railroad yard as a longshoreman. That day, he was working beneath a giant crane that was lifting boxcars to the elevated tracks in the yard. Horribly, the chain on the giant crane slipped as it was lifting a boxcar and it crashed down on him crushing him to death instantly.

Life became difficult for the Orsini family, but my oldest brother Leo took charge of the situation and by sheer guts and hard work became the chief support of the family.

Child that I was, I soon began to get excited about the approach of Christmas. I could not comprehend the agony that my mother was experiencing. I wrote a letter to Santa Claus:

> Dear Santa,
>
> I know that you are really a Saint in heaven and that you bring nice things to good kids. I have been pretty good. Please bring me an accordion, a train, and a sled. You probably know my papa because he is in heaven too. I really want him to come home for Christmas. That would be the best present. O.K.?
>
> Love,
> Joey Orsini II
>
> P.S. If you bring me my papa back you don't have to bring all that other stuff.

I mailed the letter and waited for Christmas. Christmas Eve

3

came and we all went to midnight Mass. When we got home, I searched frantically everywhere, seriously hoping that Santa had brought my papa. Of course, papa was not there. Most of the other things I had asked for were under the tree near the Nativity scene. I began to cry as I listlessly touched the presents. My mother didn't know about the letter, but her heart told her why her child was crying. She took me in her arms, tears filling her own eyes, and led me to the tiny Nativity scene beneath the Christmas tree. She picked up the small figurine of the Christ child and asked:

"Joey, do you know who this is?"

"Yes mama, baby Jesus."

"Papa is with Jesus now, Joey, because Jesus loves him, so don't cry."

I was taught that, without Jesus, life was meaningless. But I was too young to understand. The emptiness and hurt of my father's departure lasted a very long time.

We all went to Mass on Sundays but I never was really attracted by the pomp and circumstance and just didn't understand all that went on. As I got a little older and was sent to church by myself, I often sneaked away to a local candy store to while away the time that my mother thought I was spending in church. It was the insistence of my brother Oreste that compelled me to attend catechism classes and finally make my confirmation. But I never really like church, and I was afraid of priests. We called them Father, but none of them reminded me of my papa.

Until one day I came home after school and found a priest in our living room. His name was Father Dennis McKenna, a close friend of my brother Oreste, and his warm humanity completely disarmed me. I was a lonely boy, resentful that I didn't have a dad like all my friends, a dad who took me places and played ball with me. Father McKenna took a real interest in me. I knew he was for real which meant a lot to me. Father

McKenna invited me to join a club he had organized composed of youngsters my own age called the "Knights and Handmaidens of the Blessed Sacrament." He would celebrate Mass for us and talk to us about Jesus in terms we could understand. My admiration for him began to grow.

So, as a young boy, I decided that I would study for the priesthood. This raised many an eyebrow because I just didn't seem to fit into the established mold for a candidate for the priesthood. After all, I had not gone to a Catholic school, so I didn't know too much about my religion. Besides that, I wasn't a regular churchgoer and was a rather unruly kid with a mind of my own. My scholastic record was poor—I had been left back twice—and I would get a crush on any girl who smiled at me. However, I was insistent, and with the help and encouragement of my pastor, the Reverend Dominic J. Del Monte of Our Lady of the Assumption Church in Bayonne, New Jersey, I made application to the Graymoor Franciscan Fathers and was accepted into their minor seminary.

When I arrived at the seminary, it was all very strange to me. I had not ever been in a Catholic school, and here I was in a seminary. I didn't know the ropes, but I tried very hard to conform. For the most part, the priests were very understanding, but one, the Prefect of Discipline, caught me every time I was breaking a rule, and this was so often that he lost patience with me. He judged I was incorrigible where I was honestly ignorant. As a result he put the pressure on me until I began to believe that I wasn't any good. It was a difficult time for a boy of sixteen, but the Lord saw me through. After a stormy year of trying to fit into the mold, I was dismissed from the seminary because, in their judgment, I did not have a vocation.

June 1, 1954 was my seventeenth birthday. I was feeling sorry for myself because of my dismissal from the seminary so I went downtown to my parish church to see some friends. One of them was a sixteen-year-old girl by the name of Rita Ann Bauers. I had known her from "The Knights and Handmaidens of the Blessed Sacrament," but never paid attention to her. That evening, however, I discovered that Rita was an attractive and interesting young lady. I had just gotten my driver's license and was the proud owner of a 1947 Crosley station wagon. I asked her for a date and she accepted. That summer we saw each other frequently, but we were hardly ever alone. We were part of a gang of kids, three of whom have since became nuns and one a priest. At one point I realized that I loved her. I decided that this priesthood stuff was not for me and maybe someday Rita and I would marry. When I told her, Rita exclaimed, "Joe, I feel the same way, but I've decided to try the convent to become a nun." What could I say? I was disappointed but decided to wait it out.

September came and Rita entered the convent. I was shattered. But that November she came back home. I was delighted. We started to date again. Christmas drew near and I decided to buy her a ring. We were to meet at church for midnight Mass and afterwards go to her home to exchange gifts. Rita never met me at the church. Tragically, on her way to meet me, she suffered a cerebral hemorrhage. After Mass, Father Livolsi, the new assistant priest, told me what had happened and asked me to accompany him to the hospital to assist him in giving Rita the Last Rites. I couldn't believe this was happening. We went to her bed and I prayed as Father Livolsi anointed her. All of my friends joined me in church to pray for her. In my anguish I knew that if she survived the coma, she would be no more than a vegetable and I prayed that if there really was a God, that He would mercifully take her. Foolishly, I thought that God had allowed this to happen because I had decided not to continue to study for the priesthood. A few hours later Rita breathed her last. Her wake and funeral seemed to pass like an unreal dream, but she was really gone.

I fell into a deep depression and didn't know what to think. It was only the patient and kind ministry of my pastor, Father Del Monte, that saved my sanity and faith in God. I didn't fully understand what had taken place but continued to believe in the graciousness of God, because I believed that this life is a preparation for the next; or at least I wanted to believe.

I completed my high-school studies at St. Anthony's High School in Jersey City and was encouraged by my saintly pastor to try the seminary again. This time I was openly and generously accepted by the Salesian Fathers in Newton, New Jersey, and completed my first year of college with them. I then transferred to Seton Hall University where I won my bachelor's degree in classical languages with a minor in philosophy in 1960. The diocese of Camden adopted me and sent me to St. John's Home Missions Seminary in Little Rock, Arkansas, to study theology. At the same time, during summer vacations, I studied for the master's degree in education. Finally I was ordained to the priesthood on May 16, 1964, by the late Most Reverend Celestine Damiano, D.D., Archbishop-Bishop of Camden.

As a young priest I began very enthusiastically but without too much regard for my health. As a result I collapsed from nervous exhaustion and sustained some physical damage. After six years in the priesthood I became very disillusioned and bitter, especially with the hypocrisy I found in my own life and the lives of some of my ecclesiastical peers. We didn't practice what we preached. I was assigned to teach full-time at Camden Catholic High School in Cherry Hill, New Jersey, at the same time that I was assisting in various parishes within the diocese. I tried to fulfill my duties in the ministry as conscientiously as possible but knew I lacked conviction and power.

Various circumstances began to work in my life to divorce me from prayer and meditation. Since I was teaching religion, I plunged headlong into all the latest techniques and methods in religious education; but no matter what I tried, I sensed a deepening frustration within myself because I could see that what I was teaching was not really reaching the hearts or changing the lives of the boys and girls in my classes. When I began to look at this problem I tried every possible solution. I thought perhaps if I became a little less formal in class, maybe that would do it. Or perhaps if I took some classes in the teaching of scripture, that would do it. Or if I took some courses in modern catechetics, that would do it. I tried every human effort to bring Christ into that classroom and it didn't happen. Of course the real reason for my failure, the fact that Jesus Christ and I didn't have a real personal relationship, didn't occur to me, or if it did, I rejected it as too simple a solution. I knew a great deal *about* Jesus; after all, my studies in college and seminary had given me a solid philosophical and theological background, and I had continued my studies in theology day after day as a priest. Jesus Christ was the subject of my intellectual pursuit, but He had never become an existential reality in my life. I had enough of the name of Christ in my mind, but I didn't have Him in my heart. And I was too proud to realize it. After all, I was a religious leader, an ordained minister. I was a priest. And if anyone should know Jesus Christ, I thought I should.

Protestant evangelicals talk about "being saved," "a salvation experience," or "accepting Jesus Christ as a personal Savior;" what they mean in Catholic terms is making real and personal what the sacrament of baptism did for us as infants. It is the simple wholehearted acceptance of the assurance of salvation that Jesus offers to every man, and the release or surrender of our lives in trust and faith to Jesus Christ.

8

There is no particular formula or pattern that one must follow to receive this liberating experience. Only one thing is necessary, as St. Paul says in Romans 10: "You don't understand that Christ has died to make you right with God. Instead you are trying to make yourselves good enough to gain God's favor by keeping religious laws and customs, but that is not God's way of salvation. You don't understand that Christ gives to those who trust in Him everything you are trying to get by keeping His laws. He ends all that . . . . For salvation that comes from trusting Christ . . . is already within easy reach of us . . . . For if you confess with your mouth that Jesus is your Lord and believe in your heart that God has raised Him from the dead, you will be saved."

Roman Catholics do not believe that this is a once and for all experience, although its initial step can be traced to a particular time and place. It is a continual experience of gradual surrender, leading the individual into ever deeper commitment to Jesus Christ. It is the "conversion" or "metanoia" that the saints and spiritual writers have written about in our Catholic tradition for centuries. It is the necessary first step that leads you into an ever-deepening and ever-progressive identification with the life of Jesus.

But I didn't understand all of this then, and, as time went on, my frustration turned into bitterness, my pride kept me from seeking the answer in Jesus Himself and I began to experience a deep cynicism and coldness of heart. My priesthood devolved into a pseudoprofessionalism, and I began to lose my faith.

II

Down the Dark Road

Whenever I was called upon to preach or to perform the sacraments, that was exactly what I did—I performed. I began to look for excuses not to celebrate Mass, not to accept speaking engagements, not to hear confessions. When, however, I couldn't evade these duties, I performed them with great reluctance. I didn't want to really get involved. I invented all sorts of excuses: "Well, I've been teaching high school all day, and I'm tired. So let the other guy do it." What I didn't realize at that time was that I just didn't have the feeling within me; I was losing my belief.

A priest can lose his faith very easily. You see, those of us who are professional religious people become so familiar with the word of God that it becomes mechanical with us after a while. If we don't really have the spirit of God within us, it becomes a job like any other job. And this is what was happening to me.

There began a period of profound interior struggle where I didn't know who or what I was. I began to take the counsel of contemporary and older priest friends; some, reflecting their own frustration, told me that this was all I could expect of the priesthood, and others told me to pray more. I began to sincerely believe the first and refused to follow the advice of the latter, for it seemed too simplistic an answer. Eventually, I came to the point of complete disgust with corruption. I lost interest in everything religious and became hypercritical of anyone who professed belief, assigning to them my own hypocrisy. My own faith was so weak that it amounted to almost nothing.

When I talk about the corruption of the ecclesiastical system, I do not mean to condemn the whole church. I believe in the essential sanctity of the body of Christ. I believe that most priests are sincere and holy men who are trying to serve God and His people. But there are men in the priesthood who have become ensnared in hypocrisy and who climb the ladder of ecclesiastical power because they know how to play the game. As a result they damage the lambs that are theirs by virtue of their office.

I really cannot blame this state of affairs on my church or denomination because I had been repeatedly told in the seminary that unless I sought God in Jesus Christ every day in prayer and meditation I would lose my spiritual power and vitality. But in the spirit of the times and in the revolution that is taking place within the institutional church and the pseudotheology of the social gospel, I felt I was too busy to pray, too busy to meditate. And I convinced myself that God would be more pleased if I were constantly with the people taking care of their "needs." I refused to realize that the Son of God Himself, Jesus Christ, in the example of His ministry, showed clearly that any effective minister of His gospel must put time aside each day, prime time, to pray, to communicate with God the Father. This is the source of the power of the ministry.

I wrongly interpreted systematic prayer as merely another organizational procedure. It was too simple an answer, too naive. I was at a point in my intellectual life where I felt that my mind was so sharp, so sophisticated, and I understood so much, that I really had no need for the kinds of procedures that others less intellectually endowed needed. I was very suspicious about people who got emotionally involved with religion and very impatient with pious people. I became critical of good and holy priests who spent hours in prayer, and who spent much time in ministering to the sick and to the poor of their parishes, claiming that this was merely a form of escapism, particularly for those who were incapable of more intellectual pursuits. I thought they should study more theology and have a more rounded intellectual life. Little did I know they had the real secret. As a student I had read volumes on the lives of the saints and the spiritual life, all of which stressed the ultimate importance of a deep personal relationship with Christ established through prayer. So, I cannot really blame what my church *taught* for the state of my spirit, for it taught the necessity of prayer. But I was looking for a scapegoat, and so I latched on to the emptiness and corruption in the lives of some of my contemporary ecclesiastics. But the real reason why I had become stunted in my Christian growth was because I had not taken the means that were available to me to grow in the Christian life.

I finally came to the point where I had to make a decision. Many of my friends in the priesthood at this time were questioning the validity of their own vocations. Some, the older ones, decided to stick with it, for what else could they do? Others, the younger ones, were leaving. My own resolve to stay was becoming weaker and weaker. Then something happened that almost pushed me off the precipice. By circumstance I discovered the moral decay of an associate in the ministry, and panic-stricken, I saw a glimpse of what could happen to me. I didn't know where to turn. I decided that the only way I could in conscience remain in the priesthood would be to leave the system for a while. If that were not possible, then I would have to leave the priesthood altogether.

My bishop granted me a leave of absence during which I would begin a course of studies leading to the doctorate, so as not to be idle. This was in January 1970; my leave would begin in June. At that time I began to read books that weakened my faith even more, books—like *The Passover Plot*—that criticized and even denied the divinity of Jesus Christ, and finally, at one point, I fell into complete disbelief in the divinity of Christ. I believed that Jesus was paranoid, self-deluded. I had been hurt, I now realize, by the actions of some of my superiors, and so I sought to retaliate in this awful, self-destructive way.

I had reached the end of the road. I was frightened, unhappy, and empty. The final decision was made, at least in my mind. I would leave the priesthood and the church. There was nothing else I could do. With the decision, I felt a load come off my shoulders. At last I would really find what life was all about. All these years I had been on the outside, looking in, but now all that would change. I would begin by taking a little vacation.

I didn't know that Jesus had some plans of His own.

III

The Light in the Darkness

Time was passing very slowly, but when Easter vacation arrived I had a week off from my teaching duties at Paul VI High School. I decided to go to Puerto Rico and get away from it all. Before I left, I was talking to one of my priest friends in the rectory who asked me if I had ever heard of the Catholic Pentecostal movement.

"The *what* movement?" I asked

"The Catholic Pentecostal movement," he repeated.

"No, Tony," I said emphatically. "I haven't heard of any such movement, nor do I care to." *Catholic Pentecostals indeed!*

"Well," he said, "I noticed that you've been really going through it. Maybe something like that would help."

"Tony," I said impatiently, "let's talk about something else—if you don't mind."

But Tony wasn't the only person trying to crowd me into something in which I was not remotely interested. Before I left on my vacation I got a strange letter from a man I'd never heard of. It was from Father Joseph Hartman, another Catholic priest, and he was from Michigan. I wondered where he got my name. I figured it was another appeal for money—we get them all the time—and I supposed I would probably throw the letter away as soon as I read it.

The first sentence leaped out at me:

"Praise the Lord!"

Another religious kook, I thought disgustedly. I was in no mood to hear anyone say "Praise the Lord," because I had just gone through the process of denying His existence. Nevertheless, some strange compulsion made me read the letter. Father Hartman said he was led to write to me because he knew I had a troubled heart.

A troubled heart! I said to myself. *What is he, a physician making a diagnosis, or is he some kind of spiritual quack who thinks he can see into my heart–into my soul?*

In the letter he asked me if I'd ever heard the term "Catholic Pentecostal." Hearing those two words used together again almost made my hair fall out. I couldn't see it—they just didn't jibe. In my own tradition, Catholic meant order, hierarchy, government, sacrament, dignity, and quiet; Pentecostal brought visions of all kinds of "wild" jumping, shouting, tambourines, and emotionalism.

That would be an interesting animal–if such a creature existed, I had to admit, *a Catholic Pentecostal.*

My priestly correspondent went on to describe his own Pentecostal experience, and closed the letter with asking me to pray and promising that he would pray for me. Well, I wasn't going to pray; I was going to go on vacation and leave all these disturbing things behind me. But Jesus had gotten His foot in the door. And I was soon to learn that when He has His hands upon you, it doesn't matter how far you run, how deep you hide, He's still got you.

I began at once to feel uneasy about the decision I had made, but I figured the strange uncomfortableness was like indigestion—if I took the right medicine, it would go away. The right medicine would be to take my trip to Puerto Rico and forget the whole thing.

Well, I went to Puerto Rico, and I spent the most miserable seven days of my life. I could not escape this Jesus. Every single day something would happen to remind me of Him. One afternoon after the sun had set I went into a cocktail lounge to have a drink before dinner. I was sitting at the bar, drowning my sorrows, and a gentleman next to me asked, "What do you think about Jesus Christ?"

My immediate reaction was a wincing, "Oh, no! Not here, too!" A bar was the last place I expected to hear that kind of question. I rushed out without answering the man and went up to my room to shake for a while. Then I left for home on the next plane. I wanted to escape what I thought was just a bad scene.

When I got to my room in the rectory I felt safe—but not for long. There was a note on my telephone:

"Brother Panky called. Please return his call." There was a number listed, but who in the world was Brother Panky? Anybody with a name like that had to be weird. But my curiosity got the best of me and I telephoned anyway, against my better judgment.

"Hello, is this Brother Panky?" I asked.

"Yes, it is, praise the Lord!" the voice answered. I almost hung up right then. *Oh, no, I protested inwardly. Not again. Not another one of those!*

But it was too late to back out. I couldn't just hang up. I'd have to hear him out. When I told him who I was and explained that I was returning his call, he said, "Someone told me you were interested in the Catholic Pentecostal movement." I stood there in utter defeat, just shaking my head. He went on to tell me about the prayer meetings they had every Friday night and invited me to come over.

"I'll keep them in mind," I lied, and thanked him for getting in touch with me. When I hung up the phone I consigned the paper with his name and number on it to the permanent file, my wastebasket, and figured that was the end of that.

Next I turned my attention to a box that had come in the mail during my absence. The return address indicated that the package had been sent by the priest who had written to me before I went on vacation. Somewhat hesitantly I opened the package and was confronted by three books: *The Cross and the Switchblade*, by David Wilkerson; *They Speak with Other Tongues*, by John Sherrill; and *Catholic Pentecostals*, by Kevin and Dorothy Ranaghan.

I looked up and said, "What are you doing to me?" And I kind of surrendered, as if I knew that running away wasn't getting me anywhere at all. So I sat down and began to read *The Cross and the Switchblade*. As I read, the Lord touched my heart. Something happened inside me. I wanted to believe the book was true, that Jesus was real and that all you had to do was trust His Word and that signs and wonders would follow. *Wouldn't it be wonderful if this was really true!* I said inside myself.

I finished the book in about half an hour, then picked up the next one, *They Speak with Other Tongues*. That, too, gripped my attention, as did the last one of the three. About one o'clock in the morning I went to my bookshelf, dusted off my Bible and read some more. The words, words that had been dull and meaningless for so long, began to come alive to me, to jump off the page with significance for my life. I spent the night reading, and went to breakfast the next morning with a strange smile on my face. I didn't have to look in a mirror to see it; I could feel it coming out from the inside of me.

One of my fellow priests looked at me rather strangely.

"Where were you last night?" he asked with an accusing grin.

"Right here," I said, "reading my Bible."

"Yeah," he said, "yeah," and his eyebrows shot up half a mile. It was plain that he didn't think the Bible was all *that* interesting.

I didn't have time to explain, because I had to be off to school, but I knew I would talk to him later. When I got to school I settled down and rationalized a little: *Well, this was a pleasant experience, but I don't really know if it was real or not or if Jesus is real or not. I better play it cool.* And I decided not to mention it to anyone else, at least not yet.

The first person I saw that morning at school was a colleague in the religion department.

"Hey, Joe," he called out to me, "how would you like to go to a Catholic Pentecostal prayer meeting?"

I was stunned. This was too much to be another mere coincidence. I felt threatened by the purposefulness behind all these "chance" happenings. I wanted to put it off. I had become quite comfortable with my apathy, and I really didn't want anything shaking my own little world. So I told him, "No, thanks," and began making excuses in my mind:

This kind of stuff is too way-out. I don't want to go to a prayer meeting, because maybe I'll start laughing and they'll throw me out.

What I was really saying was that my apathy and emptiness had become my security blanket, and I didn't want anything to take it away. If Jesus were really to come into my life, I'd have to change too much, or I'd have to give up too much. I didn't realize then that Jesus said, "Seek ye first the Kingdom of God . . . and all these things will be added unto you." The only things Jesus asks us to leave behind are things that are no good for us, things that are illicit, immoral, dragging us down, emptying us, and weakening us. "All these things will be added unto you," means that Jesus will take care of all our needs. But I didn't know that at the time.

That evening when I arrived at the rectory for supper, there was a note for me to call a number at Cherry Hill Hospital. The young man who answered identified himself as David Patrick, one of my former students. He was about to undergo

19

open-heart surgery and wanted to receive the sacraments before he went into the operating room. I went to the hospital that evening, still in a state of confusion of mind myself, and heard his confession, then took him Holy Communion early the next morning, right before his scheduled surgery.

Open-heart surgery is the most atrocious assault the surgeons can make upon the human body. It's an awful thing, with a painful postoperative procedure also, and it's very dangerous. I knew that. And this boy, only twenty-one, asked me to help him pray. As we were praying together, the attendants came to wheel him up to surgery. He was apprehensive and asked if I could be with him when he regained consciousness. Permission was granted.

When I came away from that place I realized that this was exactly what God had been wanting me to do in my ministry. This was what I had been missing all my life, bringing Jesus to others. The reason why I hadn't brought Him to others was because I hadn't known Him myself. I went back to the rectory having promised David I would be present when he got out of surgery.

Well, I was there, and what I saw made me feel so helpless, because here was this poor boy who already had a broken marriage, and who had all kinds of problems. Here he was, lying helpless, with tubes coming out of him. I'm a coward to begin with; I can't stand pain even when I see it in others. My first impulse was to run out as soon as I could, but something kept me there until his eyes opened. He looked at me, unable to say a word, but those pain-wracked eyes screamed, "Help me! Help me!" Only I was helpless too. I didn't know what to do, what to say. Because I wasn't baptised in the Holy Spirit then, I didn't know about the laying on of hands; I didn't know that Jesus would truly answer our prayers.

I couldn't bear to stay, but blurted out, "I'm going to go to a prayer meeting for you," and rushed from the room.

Now I had really done it. I had committed myself to go to a Catholic Pentecostal prayer meeting.

I learned there was such a meeting the very next night at St. Boniface Church on Diamond Street in Philadelphia. The next evening, Friday, April 10, found me with two of my high-school boys, Anthony Panichella and Joe Angelastro, entering the doors at St. Boniface for our first prayer meeting.

When we walked into the church, we saw thirty to forty people, all smiling warmly and greeting us as if we were long-lost brothers. They seemed so happy that I thought maybe it was a put-on. Then I saw a smiling cherub of a man whom everyone was calling "Panky." His name was Brother Pancratius Boudreau, C.S.S.R., the spiritual leader of this Catholic Pentecostal community. He welcomed me very graciously, and we entered the room where the prayer meeting was to be held.

They began singing some very lively songs, and before long I relaxed and joined in, even clapping my hands and stomping my feet, sharing their enthusiasm. After a time, Brother "Panky" asked all those who were there for the first time to go into another room for a First-Nighters' talk. There were three or four of us.

Brother Panky went with us to an office-like room where he walked over to a big Bible and began to read. As he read, the Word began to speak to my heart. At first it made me uneasy, this simple man reading the Bible and explaining it in his very simple terms. But then my heart began to melt. And I knew that something was going to happen to me that night. He talked to us a little about the charismatic gifts, and everything he said made sense to me, theoretically.

We moved back into the church, then, and lined up before the altar along with the other people. I heard them praying freely, with such boldness of faith, and with such an outpouring of thankfulness for all the wonderful things that Jesus had done

21

for them in the past week, that my own faith was greatly strengthened. I had always prayed, "IF it be Thy Will," "IF maybe, perhaps," and never positively, "Lord, thank you for doing this."

But as I stood there, hearing their prayers of faith and thanksgiving, the words poured out of me. I couldn't hold them back. I began to pray for David, that he would be so well that there would be no mistake about it, that it would have to be acknowledged as a miracle. I had never prayed with such boldness before.

Then an announcement was made that if anyone needed prayer for personal needs he should kneel at the altar, and the members of the community would lay hands on him and pray. I knelt and made my peace with Jesus; I asked Him to forgive me for my lack of faith and to come into my heart. Brother Panky stood in front of me and Helen Dickerson stood behind. They laid hands on me and Panky began to pray in English. He then asked my request, and I asked for the baptism in the Holy Spirit (that special infilling with the Holy Spirit that confers the charismatic gifts mentioned in I Cor. 12). Brother Panky began to pray in Greek (I didn't know then that this was a manifestation of the gift of tongues) and I had a definite exalting experience. Tears began to stream down my face, and my whole body trembled. When I got up, I knew that this was not merely an emotional experience, that something real had happened. It was April 10, 1970. My new life in Christ had begun.

IV

Signs and Wonders

The next day I went to the hospital to see how the young man was doing. I didn't want to go. Because if he was healed, I'd have to move into this whole experience, and my life would be completely changed. And if he wasn't healed—then what?

I drove to the hospital with great trepidation. I walked into his room, and he wasn't there. I asked the nurse where he was, fearing he had died.

"I don't know where that young man is," she said. "I thought maybe *you* could tell *me*." It seems that he had been up, walking up and down the hall, although open-heart surgery patients usually stayed in bed for two weeks, and he had had his operation only two days earlier!

I found him in the coffee shop.

"What's going on here?" I asked him, utterly amazed at how well he looked.

"I don't know, I really don't know," he confessed. "But I know that God is doing something for me."

"Well, can you tell me what happened?" I croaked at him, so overwhelmed I could hardly speak.

"Sure, I can tell you. It started in the night. I couldn't sleep.

I was in terrible pain. And I heard a voice—within—tell me, 'Sleep now. You're going to be all right.' I believed it, and I slept. Then about three or four o'clock in the morning I heard somebody saying, 'David, get up.' It was preposterous, of course, and I thought it was the guy next to me talking. It kind of made me mad, so I just snuggled down under the covers.

"Then I heard the voice again, louder this time, saying the same thing, so I yelled, 'Shut up, will you?' and I opened my eyes to glare at the fellow in the next bed. But he was sound asleep.

"The next time the voice came it was *very* forceful, and I was wide awake. There was no mistaking what it said:

" 'David, get up and *walk.*'

"I felt as if two hands got behind me and pushed me right out of that bed.

"Father, I don't know what's happening, but whatever it is, it's wonderful."

I had listened to his account with my mouth hanging wide open in amazement. I had prayed for a miracle. A miracle had happened. I didn't say it out loud, but I was thinking, "Praise the Lord."

The following Tuesday evening found me back at St. Boniface for a closed core meeting of the Pentecostal community. There was no reluctance in me this time. As I related the remarkably improved condition of the young man, no one seemed surprised. All the people were confident that the patient had been healed by the divine intervention of God. Indeed, just a week from the day he was operated on, the young man was dismissed from the hospital, his recovery "unexplainably complete."

No longer did I think about leaving; no longer did I think about what was wrong with the church; but I began to seek Jesus Christ and to know Him more.

A few days later I was informed that my ten-year-old nephew

24

was seriously ill with pneumonia; in fact, his condition was critical. I went home, expecting the worst, but Jesus used this situation to bring glory to His name. Although the doctor had given up all hope, we prayed for his healing—and my nephew was healed.

On April 28, 1970, I was again at a prayer meeting at St. Boniface; I was attending twice a week now. It was while I was sitting in proxy for the continued healing of my nephew that the Holy Spirit came upon me and gave me the gift of tongues—a blessed gift I use each day in prayer as the Holy Spirit directs.

With all these blessings occurring, June came quickly, and I began my leave of absence. I went back to Bayonne, New Jesey, to live at my own home, assist my pastor in the parish, and begin my doctoral studies.

No one at home knew of my Pentecostal experience except a few members of my family and my pastor and friend, Father Del Monte. But everyone knew that there was something different about me—a new vitality, a new honesty. And every Friday during the month of June I was making a 160-mile round trip to St. Boniface in Philadelphia for a prayer meeting. Finally one day Father Del Monte and I were talking about the Pentecostal movement and he said, "Joe, I know that there is really something wonderful and valid about all this because I can see the great change it has made in you. Why don't we start having prayer meetings right here, in our parish?"

This was an answer to my secret longing, an invitation to form a Pentecostal community on my home grounds. I went into immediate action and called Brother Panky to come to Bayonne to help us get started. One evening in July, Brother Panky, Joe Mallon, Helen Dickerson, Kay and Nick Adams, and their daughters all drove up to Bayonne in a Volkswagen bus. At Our Lady of Assumption Church we had assembled about thirty interested people who didn't know what to expect. Brother Panky began the prayer meeting by invoking the precious Blood of Jesus to protect us all from satanic forces. He prayed that the Holy Spirit would come upon us all in a warm manifestation of His love and power. All of the "veterans" in the movement shared their insights; we prayed and really felt the presence of the Lord. It was a rather quiet meeting, however, no speaking in tongues, no prophecy, and it came to an official close after about an hour.

Then it happened! Regina Bachely, a registered nurse who had come to the meeting only to please a friend, was moved to come up to Brother Panky and myself to ask for a prayer of deliverance from occult bondage. She was worried because she had become rather involved with tarot cards, an ouija board, astrology, and all the counterfeit tricks of the devil. Panky and I prayed a simple prayer of exorcism, followed by a prayer in faith that the Holy Spirit would take rightful possession of this child of God. Regina suddenly came under the power of the Holy Spirit and startled herself and everyone around by immediately praising God with the gift of tongues. That did it! Everyone there saw a live example of what we had been talking about.

The merely curious never returned. It was all right talking about these things on the theoretical level, but when they actually saw and heard the gifts of the Holy Spirit in action, they felt threatened. Others became convinced of the reality of God's presence and from this nucleus the Bayonne Catholic Pentecostal community was born.

We met every Friday night and had from seventy to eighty, sometimes a hundred people, and the Lord blessed the Bayonne Catholic Pentecostal community with many healings and prophecies. In fact, I myself was healed of total deafness in the left ear, and a woman was cured of cancer of the spine, a girl was delivered from an evil spirit, and personal relationships were healed through the prayers of Spirit-filled Christians. There were many other wonderful manifestations of Jesus' presence.

The Lord showed us through prophecy that we are to be a living sign of His Divine Love. We came to recognize that we were truly brothers and sisters and that the love of Jesus bound us together to form a community through which Christ was and is renewing His churches.

- Invoke precious Blood of Jesus to protect from satanic power

- pray for Holy Spirit to come upon us

The Baptism of the Holy Spirit

If you are a Catholic reading this little book, you are probably asking yourself this question: "Is it for me?" You are probably also wondering if all this fits in with the teachings of the Catholic church. Perhaps the following will help to answer your questions. It comes from an article, "The Essential Element in the Church," by Kevin Ranaghan, a theologian from Notre Dame University:

"The Catholic church very often looks to the day of Pentecost as to its beginning. Jesus, having finished His work on earth, was now seated at the Father's right hand in glory. The wonderful act of redemption for all time had taken place. Yet Jesus wanted his saving love to endure throughout history. He wanted His Word, His life, His love and His salvation to be available to men in all generations and in all places. Therefore, He left behind Him a group of believers to communicate the mystery of His love. It's very interesting to look at that small band of believers gathered together in Jerusalem, behind closed doors in an upper room. They were the people who had been very close to the Lord, who had lived with Him for three years. They believed in Him, but their faith was something that they shared only among themselves, they had no active outgoing ministry to the world. Yet Jesus had told them, "As the Father sent me, so I send you.' Then came the day of Pentecost when the Father and Jesus, fully anointed as Christ and Lord, sent the Holy Spirit into that band of 120 believers, and they were transformed and enlivened with power. What happened in that upper room was that Jesus, who had been with them in His risen body forty days after the resurrection and was now seated at the right hand of the Father, made His presence known and felt among them by the power of His Holy Spirit. The Spirit came upon that group and filled them with the most wonderful awareness of the presence of Jesus in their midst. The results of this are evidenced by what they did. True, there was the sound of the rushing wind and tongues as of fire and the speaking in tongues, but note the effect of this outpouring of the Holy Spirit. They immediately began to preach the gospel effectively with such power that on that first day three thousand or so believed. Transformed into the mystical body of Christ and made one in the Holy Spirit, those believers could now go forth as an historical extension of Jesus Christ to effectively preach His gospel and communicate as He acts through them."

That is what happened on Pentecost when the church was born. This is a standard Catholic approach to the subject. Without the Holy Spirit, without Pentecost, there is no church. It is the life of the Spirit that is the very heart of the life of the church. The coming of the Holy Spirit was absolutely essential in order that there be any church at all.

The same thing is true on the individual level. Catholics become members of the mystical body of Christ through three rites or sacraments of initiation, rites that incorporate someone who is outside the body of Christ, into the life of Christ. These sacraments are: baptism with water, confirmation, and Holy Communion—the celebration of the Lord's Supper. These rites bring a person from a state outside the church (which is not so much outside an organization as outside a sharing of the life of Jesus), into a sharing of the life of the Spirit, which is to say into the sharing of the life of Jesus. Again the point is this: it is the action of the Holy Spirit in baptism, confirmation, and the eucharist that takes a person and involves him in the death and resurrection of Jesus, and that brings him in with Jesus to that point where he can say, "Abba, Father." Thus, on both the community and individual levels, the life of the Holy Spirit is absolutely essential for there to be any Christianity at all.

When we talk about the life of the Spirit—about receiving the Holy Spirit—we are talking about such a fantastic and wonderful reality that our minds aren't capable of fully comprehending it. We often speak of the Holy Spirit as the personal expression of the love relationship between the Father and the Son. God is love, we are told in the Word; His very life is His love. Love is at the heart of God's life, and the Holy Spirit is the expression, the embodiment, of that love dwelling in our midst.

The phrase, "the baptism in the Holy Spirit," used simply in its literal sense, speaks of an immersion or a plunging of the individual into the life stream of the Spirit of Christ. Some come into this experience in a prayer group where there is a ministry of the laying on of hands, but this is not at all essential. Some people experience the baptism by themselves—at home, where they work, or in some other place. It is neither a rite nor a sacrament; it's simply Jesus keeping His promise to pray the Father to pour out His Holy Spirit on those who believe. Jesus is seated at the right hand of the Father, loving the Father eternally with the same love with which He loved the Father on Calvary. Together they are still pouring out the Holy Spirit upon the Church. This is a timeless activity, a timeless promise, and God must indeed be true to His Word.

From the point of view of the believer, however, the baptism

31

in the Holy Spirit is an occasion, or a moment, of explicit and radical faith. An individual who comes to receive the baptism in the Holy Spirit realizes that the Lord "wills" to pour out His Spirit and power upon all who believe. It is not a case of "Wouldn't it be nice if Jesus would pour out His Spirit," or, "If I pray, maybe Jesus will pour out His Spirit and renew the gifts of the Spirit in me." No! It's a moment of faith in which the individual says, "Jesus has promised this to the whole Church, to all the members of His body, and that includes me. This is meant to be a norm for the Christian life and is to be believed and accepted in faith."

The person coming to receive the baptism in the Holy Spirit has this attitude, "Lord I believe so much and so simply, that I expect as I pray that you are renewing me in the Holy Spirit as you promised."

The results can be categorized on two different levels: First of all, on the level of individual spiritual life, interior faith life. On this level there is a change, a transformation, a tremendous deepening of the life of faith. Many people express it this way: "The Lord Jesus came so close to me by the power of the Spirit, and I experienced Him personally in such an intimate union of love that my faith life has been totally renewed. My confidence in Him, and in the whole reality of the Christian life, has been renewed through and through."

In this new relationship of love there is produced in the life of the individual what we call the fruit of the Holy Spirit—love, peace, joy, long-suffering, gentleness, goodness, meekness, and temperance. That is to say the qualities of Christ, the attributes of His life, are shared by the believer who has encountered Him by the power of the Holy Spirit. People suddenly find themselves in love with God and very concretely in love with the members of their family, with the people with whom they work, with the people in their community. They find themselves so filled with this love, so full of joy and peace, that they instinctively want to communicate it so that others may share in it.

The second level of experience is on the community or the group level. Here are experiences which are called the gifts of the Holy Spirit, the ministry gifts, spoken of by St. Paul in I Cor. 12. Some of the people who receive the baptism in the Holy Spirit have a new and uncanny ability to see into the lives of other people, to recognize the influences of good and evil. Others receive the discernment of spirits. They find themselves seeing the problems and needs of others, and they possess the ability to speak a word to them that meets that problem directly or to offer a word of advice or encouragement, exhortation, or rebuke that serves as a tool to lead another person closer to Christ. They begin to experience gifts of healing—not just physical healing but total personal healing. They begin to experience on the psychological level and on the personal level the healing of deep wounds within them, or the healing of broken relationships within their families and among their friends. They begin to experience physical healing too.

Perhaps you, like me, have been raised with the idea that physical healing is a rare occurrence in the church, that the "hoot and holler" type of healing service that we sometimes hear over the radio or see on television is some sort of a circus act. As a result of that, we are very prone to reject healing and to think that it doesn't really happen. Yet many people who had thought this way begin to experience physical healing. Through a prayer of faith, a disease which was physically present, is suddenly gone. Some begin also to experience other gifts of the Spirit, of being moved to speak in the community a word from the Lord and to prophesy. They receive the gift of praising God in a new and strange language which they themselves do not understand but which they find increases their prayer life in depth and meaning, builds up their faith, and gives them confidence to go on in the life of witness and ministry to other people.

Some of these gifts of the Holy Spirit may strike the twentieth-century American as weird, other-worldly, and even perhaps as superstition. But note that these gifts are not rewards for leading a good Christian life. They do not come through much learning. They are not "battle ribbons" handed out by Christ to elite Christians. Not at all! As a matter of fact, the gifts of the Holy Spirit are given for the fuller life of the Christian community. They are given so that the gospel may be preached more effectively, the needs of the community met, the kingdom of God built up here and now, and the individual built up in faith. Note how clearly Paul speaks of these as different ministries, functions, and operations of the one Spirit of Jesus Christ. That is to say, if in a group there is healing, or if there is prophecy, or if there is discernment of spirits, it is not the individual who is a healer, prophet, or discerner. It is that activity of Jesus' ministry when He was on earth 2,000 years ago that continues today through the members of His body ministering to each other to the building up of the Church.

VI

The Gifts of the Holy Spirit

One very important thing I am learning in this new experience with Jesus is that He is really faithful to His Word. It is recorded in the Gospel according to Mark, that right before Jesus ascended into heaven He told His disciples, "You are to go into all the world and preach the Good News to everyone, everywhere. Those who believe and are baptized will be saved. But those who refuse to believe will be condemned. And those who believe shall use My authority to cast out demons, and they shall speak new languages . . . and they will be able to place their hands on the sick and heal them."

I have experienced all these things that Jesus promised in operation in my own life and in the lives of other Christians who have had the baptism in the Holy Spirit. However, I have also learned that Jesus continues to minister to His people in these spectacular ways only where there is the expectancy of faith, either on the part of the person who ministers in Jesus' name or on the part of the recipient of the ministry. Bold and unwavering faith is the key to the abundant life in the Holy Spirit.

In March 1971 I received a telephone call from Father Edward Schott, T.O.R., a teacher of religion at Bishop Egan High School in Levittown, Pennsylvania. I knew Father Ed from my many contacts with him in the Catholic Pentecostal community at St. Boniface in Philadelphia.

When I answered the telephone he sounded exuberant: "Praise the Lord! Hi, Joe! How are you doing?" he asked.

"Fine, Ed," I answered. "I'm keeping very busy with my classes and work at Rutgers, and our community in Bayonne is doing great. The Lord is really blessing us."

"Joe, we are going to have a two-day retreat at our school," he went on, after commenting on my activities, "and I would like to know if you can accept the job of running it for us."

I swallowed hard, wondering if this was something I should attempt. "Well, Ed, I really don't know," I told him. "How many students do you have there?"

He answered immediately. "We have 1400 boys here, and we really would like to get them on fire with the love of Jesus."

That sounded like a worthwhile goal, all right. But I'd need some time—

"Ed," I sparred, "let me pray about it to see how the Lord directs—then I'll call you in a couple of days. Okay?"

"Yeah, sure, that's great," he agreed. "We'll be praying here too. Let me know as soon as you can."

That night we had a leadership meeting of the Bayonne Catholic Pentecostal community, and together we sought the will of the Lord in prayer. After a brief period of silence the Lord made His will known through prophecy that He wanted our community to step out in faith and respond to the call for assistance. He promised that He would work in marvelous ways to confirm the preaching of His Word. That was all I needed. The next day I called Father Ed and accepted the invitation to conduct the retreat.

I drove to Bishop Egan High School on a Monday afternoon.

The retreat was to be held on the following Tuesday and Wednesday. I was very graciously welcomed by Father Ed and Father Bob, two priests on the faculty who had received the baptism in the Holy Spirit. After supper that evening, Father Bob asked me to accompany him to the prayer meeting of the teen-age Catholic Pentecostal prayer community which had been organized by the boys at Bishop Egan.

This was the first time I had been in attendance at a teen-age prayer meeting, and I was deeply moved at the sight of normal, healthy teen-age boys, about fifteen of them, opening themselves up to Jesus. They were so filled with love for one another and for Jesus that the Lord blessed them with an abundance of the charismatic gifts. It was a beautiful thing to see and hear teen-age boys getting up without shame or embarrassment to give their personal testimony of how they had found Jesus in a wonderful experience with the Holy Spirit. They spoke of how they had become better Catholics because of this experience, how now they loved to pray, to read and study scripture to participate in the celebration of the Eucharist, and to take advantage of the Sacrament of Penance. In other words, they felt such a hunger for God in Jesus Christ, that they were almost compelled to use all the means of honoring Jesus that have developed in the Catholic church through the centuries. They were so obviously filled with the joy of the Lord that their very faces were transformed and glowing. The prayer meeting came to a close and Father Bob and I drove back to the monastery attached to the high school. After prayer together to ask the Lord's blessing for the next two days, I retired.

The next morning I awoke early to prepare the talks I would give. After Mass and breakfast I walked over to the school. I went into the large auditorium at 9:00 A.M. and the retreat officially opened. Standing behind a podium on the stage, I looked out to see about seven hundred seniors and juniors. I began with a short prayer, and nervously commenced my prepared talk. I could see they were daring me to interest them. Inwardly I moaned, "Oh, what did I get myself into?" After about ten minutes I realized they weren't listening—I had lost my audience. So I stopped, and remembering that the Lord had promised that the Holy Spirit would assist us as to what to say, I made an act of faith and claimed that promise.

I discarded my prepared talk and began to speak as the Lord directed. I really don't remember what I said, but the Lord must have used me because I sensed that not only were the students listening with their ears, but with their hearts as well. And I knew I had found the secret to the ministry—complete dependence upon Jesus Christ. Because once we start thinking the kingdom of God depends upon us, we're off the track. What He asks us to do is to empty ourselves so that He can work through us.

We broke for lunch, but not before inviting the boys to come to the gym for a short prayer meeting. When I got to the gym, I was disappointed; only about twenty out of the seven hundred showed up. But we had the little prayer meeting and really felt the presence of the Lord. All the boys who had come confessed that they really knew Jesus had been present in and with us.

In the afternoon, the Lord took over again as I preached a modern version of the parable of the prodigal son. We then celebrated the Eucharist together, and at 3:00 P.M. the first day was over. Father Ed and Father Bob assured me it was a great success, but I wasn't really convinced. That evening we came together for extended prayer, beseeching the Lord to really take over the next day.

The next morning I felt quite confident that the Lord would use that day for His glory. We followed the same schedule, this time for seven hundred sophomores and freshmen, and this time, the presence of Jesus became very real to everyone. The invitation to the little prayer meeting in the gym was accepted with wholehearted response. When I walked into the gym there were almost one hundred boys present. We began the prayer meeting, and boy after boy met the Lord in a wonderful way. During the course of the meeting a teaching was given on the promises that Jesus gave to those who believed in the gospel. Then a call was given for the laying on of hands. I went over to the side of the gym and waited. A boy of about fifteen came up to me and said, "Father, do you really believe that Jesus can do anything?"

"Yes, I do!" I answered.

"Well, so do I. Will you pray with me that the Lord will heal my left arm?"

"What's the problem with your arm?" I asked him.

"I had polio when I was little. It's been paralyzed for a long time, and I can't use it. My fingers just don't move." I noticed his arm hanging limp beside him.

About this time the other boys came up and made a circle around us, watching silently. It would be a real test of faith.

"Pray with me that Jesus will heal you right now," I told the young man, taking his lifeless left hand in mine. I began to pray, believing the promise of Jesus ". . . and they will be able to place their hands on the sick and heal them." All of a sudden, I was moved to command, "Grasp my hand! You are healed in Jesus' name."

He raised his left arm and grasped my hand tightly over and over again, crying tears of real joy. The Lord was faithful to His promise. Almost automatically, all the boys who had seen this miracle take place before their own eyes began to cry out praising Jesus.

Well, that did it. The story spread like wildfire. So many boys wanted to be ministered to with the laying on of hands, that after the afternoon session and celebration of the Eucharist, we had to arrange for another prayer meeting. The boys were officially dismissed, but so many remained in the auditorium that I called for assistance for the laying on of hands. Father Ed, Father Bob, Father Richard, Brother Tim, and I ministered to that crowd of boys for more than an hour. The Lord led us to cast out demons, to heal, and to pray for the baptism in the Holy Spirit. Every one of those boys received immediately what he had been seeking from the Lord. It was Jesus and Jesus alone who honored the faith He found in those boys. What happened to them can happen to anyone who approaches Jesus in faith.

In St. Paul's first letter to the Corinthians, he explains the nature and purpose of the gifts of the Holy Spirit. In chapter 12 he lists the gifts that can be yours for the asking:

1. The ability to give wise advice, or the word of widsom
2. The ability to say the right word to someone who is seeking the will of the Lord, or the word of knowledge
3. Special faith to act in a special need
4. The power to heal the sick
5. The power to perform miracles
6. The power to prophesy, that is, the ability to be used by the Lord to guide and direct His people
7. Discernment of spirits—the power to know whether evil spirits are speaking—the power to know whether evil spirits are speaking through those who claim to be giving God's message
8. The gift of tongues—the ability to pray in languages not learned in the normal manner
9. Interpretation of tongues—the power to understand the manifestation of tongues to the profit of the community

All or some of these gifts can be yours to be used for the glory of God and the extension of the kingdom of Jesus Christ. If you feel a lack of power and conviction in your life as a Christian and would like to have *all* that Jesus has to give you, then why not seriously investigate the claims of people who are experiencing the power of God in their lives? Do not be afraid that by seeking the Pentecostal experience you will be joining a denomination. The Pentecostal experience, the baptism in the Holy Spirit, is an *experience*, not a denomination. And the gifts are from God.

I remember that as a young man in college I became intensely interested in the whole topic of demonic and dark powers. I tried to get every available publication on this subject and became very "expert," meaning, I knew a little more than anyone else in my crowd about it. In the lives of the saints there was almost always mention of the horrible encounters with the powers of evil, and I began to wonder what all this strange stuff meant. About half of the commentaries led me to hold that all this talk of devils and witchcraft was merely the product of hysterical imaginations; yet the other half led me to suspect the reality of experiences with satanic forces.

Something happened to me that made me know the truth. The year was 1959 and the occasion was my first trip to Italy. I had traveled to Italy as a companion and interpreter for a priest who had business there with a Vatican agency. The first night in Rome we were staying at the Grand Hotel, and at about eleven I retired for the evening. I fell into a very deep sleep, but at some hour in the deadness before dawn I was abruptly awakened by the sense of some dreadful presence in the room. I was lying in bed and sensed this horrible presence coming nearer and nearer. When I tried to move, I couldn't. I fell into panic, but couldn't do anything, for I was so frightened I was virtually paralyzed. Then in the predawn dimness of that room, my eyes caught sight of a despicable-looking animal form coming closer to me. I opened my mouth to scream, but nothing came out. Then this "thing" brushed against my right arm. At that moment I screamed out the name of Jesus and it was all over. "It" simply disappeared.

My scream had roused the priest sleeping in the other bed, and when he had put on the lights, he found me almost faint with fear. He tried to comfort me by saying I was probably overtired and the whole thing was just a bad dream. We prayed for a while, and soon I calmed down. Since it was about 4:00 A.M., we decided to try to get some more sleep.

When daylight came and I had been awake for a few minutes, the whole thing came back to me, but I put it out of my mind as just a bad dream. I got up, walked into the bathroom, and prepared to shave. I was looking into the mirror, and as I lifted up my right arm to was my face, I saw it—a deep bleeding gash that ran from my elbow to my wrist. I called to my priest companion to take a look. He ran in, looked, and was dumbfounded. We tried to find every rational or natural explanation for it, even to ripping my bed apart looking for a sharp edge or object, but we found nothing. It was just an unexplainable accident—or was it?

Some years later, I was in the seminary preparing to be ordained to the order of exorcist. In my studies I learned that the Chruch has always believed in the power of the devil and provided for the distinct order of exorcist to take dominion over the power of the devil in Jesus' name. The horrible thing that had happened to me was brought back to my memory, but I just put it out of my mind.

Later, when I received the baptism in the Holy Spirit, I was so filled with peace and joy that I couldn't be bothered with thinking about these unpleasant subjects. But, as the Lord would have it, I planned to go to a charismatic conference in Pittsburgh, Pennsylvania, with Brother Panky. One of the conference teachers was a Dr. Hobart Freeman, pastor of a church in Claypool, Indiana, author of *Angels of Light?* whose topic was "Occult Bondage and Deliverance." Dr. Freeman traced the scriptural teaching on the subject and shared some of his own harrowing experiences. It was then that I realized that the devil is real and personal, a being who "as a roaring lion goes around seeking whom he may devour." It was no longer conjecture or hysteria, but a reality to contend with, as Paul writes in his letter to the Ephesians: "For we are not contending against flesh and blood, but against the principalities, against the powers, against the world rulers of this present darkness, against the spiritual hosts of wickedness." I realized that my own experience was more than an "unexplainable accident."

I write this not to frighten anyone, but to show the devil as the sham he is. Jesus Christ has given us victory over the devil and his forces, but Christians, even those who have been filled with the Holy Spirit, may, because of ignorance, fall into old Slue-Foot's traps. The devil is usually quite content with the way we live, but when we begin to take Jesus Christ seriously and claim the victory that is ours in Christ, the devil gets nervous and tries to frighten us away from the Lord. The first thing he usually does is to try to cast doubts upon our experience with Jesus. Or, he will try to attack us in that place or condition where we were weakest, for example, fear, depression, deceit, complaining, lust, or uncharitableness. But we don't have to suffer these attacks, for Satan is a defeated foe. All we have to do is ask Jesus to protect us by virtue of His blood. Satan may try to fight back, but don't let that fool you—just keep on claiming the victory in Christ and the devil will have to run.

St. Paul advises us in Ephesians, "Therefore take the whole armor of God, that you may be able to withstand in the evil day, and having done all, to stand. Stand, therefore, having girded your loins with truth, and having put on the breastplate of righteousness, and having shod your feet with the equipment of the gospel of peace, above all taking the shield of faith, with which you can quench all the flaming darts of the evil one. And take the helmet of Salvation, and the sword of the Spirit, which is the word of God. Pray at all times in the Spirit, with all prayer and supplication."

Many of those who have been involved in the charismatic renewal have long been aware of the existence and workings of the devil. But with the 1974 box office hit, *The Exorcist*, demons, demonization* and exorcism have suddenly become *the* topics of interest among the general public.

Informal exorcism or prayer for deliverance are ordinary occurrences at charismatic prayer meetings and the recent publicity given to *The Exorcist* has intensified questions concerning the actuality of the devil and diabolical activity. Since I am deeply involved in the charismatic renewal and have had some experiences with dramatic incidences of praying for deliverance, many have asked me to sum up Catholic thought and practice on exorcism. I believe that this should be done, especially to help dispel some of the false notions stirred up by the movie.

Father Donald R. Campion wrote in *America* (Feb. 2, 1974) "the Church has always recognized the possibility of possession, that is, the invasion of a personality by an alien spirit that seizes control of the personality and displaces normal human consciousness." He added, "Although there are no instances of diabolical possession in the Old Testament, there are a number of dramatic confrontations portrayed in the New Testament between Jesus and evil spirits who dominate another's body. Jesus is triumphant in these conflicts, driving the demons away.

"Similarly, there have always been Church rituals for exorcism, not only the extraordinary kind of ritual enacted in the film, but more familiar appeals that occur, for example, in the blessing of water and in the baptism of a new Christian."

The prayer of exorcism found in the Catholic rite of baptism follows a short litany invoking the saints on behalf of the welfare of the individual to be baptized. The new ritual directs the celebrant to pray: "Almighty and ever-living God, You sent Your only Son into the world to cast out the power of Satan, spirit of evil, to rescue man from the kingdom of darkness, and bring him into the splendor of Your kingdom of light. We pray for this child: set him free from orignial sin, make him a temple of Your glory, and send Your Holy Spirit to dwell with him. We ask this through Christ our Lord. *Amen.*"

The Church has become increasingly wary of designating instances of demonization. Father Campion in the article quoted, explained the Church's reasoning: "this scepticism is based not only on increased medical and scientific knowledge, but also on genuine insight."

Linda Blair's graphic portrayal of a young girl possessed by a devil in *The Exorcist* is based on an actual case that occurred in 1949. The real victim was a fourteen-year-old boy, the son of a middle-income family in the Washington suburb of Mt. Rainier, Maryland.

From an account of what took place, strange things began to happen to the boy in January 1949. His bed shook and rose into the air, a rug on which he was standing slowly slid six feet and during the actual exorcism he raged loudly and shouted obscenities in unnatural sounding voices. Along with these signs, diabolical activity and infestation took place in the boy's room and home. There were strange scratching noises in the walls, at various times objects flew around rooms and furniture suddenly raised and moved itself. The actual exorcism took place in St. Louis over a two-month period. It finally ended Easter Monday, April 18, 1949. The expulsion was so violent at times that it took ten priests to hold the boy down. Unlike the film in which two priests lose their lives, no priest died during the exorcism.

According to traditional Christian faith, demons are fallen angels who have rebelled against God. Their power is limited by God, but they retain the ability to act upon man and the material universe for their evil purposes. The form of demonic activity in which we are interested happens when a demon takes control of the personality of the individual person. Describing this in terms of a ship, the devil assumes the role of the pilot who steers the vessel. Pope Benedict XIV stated in a private opinion that "demons, in the individuals whom they possess, are like motors within the bodies which they move, but in such a way that they impress no quality on the human body nor do they give it any new mode of existence, nor . . . do they constitute, together with the possessed person, a single being."

Throughout history the Church has been reserved and cautious about reports of demonization. Such caution and hesitancy does not reflect a lack of belief in the reality of Satan and the power of evil in the world, but rather a desire correctly to identify where the evil is at work, what is natural and what is truly supernatural. For example, in themselves, spastic movements of the body or hysterical convulsions are not in themselves evidence that a person is possessed.

In the seventeenth century, a Jesuit theologian, P. Thyraus, gave four signs to determine the difference between the true demonization and natural mental phenomena. They are:

1. Revealing the hidden past or future events through the victim, which facts are shameful and scandalous in nature.
2. Speaking fluently in a foreign language the victim has never studied. (Here we must distinguish between the charismatic gift of tongues which produces the good fruit of the awareness of God's Holy Spirit and the counterfeit tongue-speaking produced by the devil with the effects of spiritual devastation—author's note.)
3. Levitation of the victim, uncontrollable body movements increasing the sense of presence of evil.
4. Telepathy and clairvoyance which bring humiliation and scandal.

Many authorities on the subject mention another criterion, namely, lack of memory as to what is said or done during the seizure. In other words, demonization involves suspension of normal human consciousness.

Cases involving the molestation of individuals, the bombarding of persons, their houses, rooms, furniture and animals have been recorded since the Middle Ages but the Church has never come easily to the conclusion that these have been genuine diabolical phenomena. The instructions of the old Roman ritual insist that every possible investigation be made for natural explanations before attributing such actions to supernatural or diabolical sources. The authorization of the bishops for the formal rite of exorcism demands exhaustive proof that the actions are not the result of natural causes. Fear-induced nightmares from seeing *The Exorcist* hardly qualify for formal exorcism.

The Church has always recognized the possibility of diabolical intervention in human lives, but insists that evil is primarily personal. Archbishop Leo Byrne of Minneapolis recently stated that "it is sin, not Satan, that is the root of all evil. Where Satan finds no complicity in evil through sin, he is powerless against us." (It is interesting to note that in *The Exorcist* the possessed girl is unbaptized and sinned against the first commandment by the use of the ouija board.) The main message here is that baptized Christians with a living and productive faith in the Lord need not fear Satan or his tricks.

With *The Exorcist* playing in neighborhood theaters, one thing is happening. Troubled people of all ages are calling priests because they are disturbed with excessive fear about the devil and possible possession. For most of these, it is unresolved sin in their lives that is the real problem. Jesus is the only solution to that problem.

Why the movie? Author William Peter Blatty expresses it this way: "*The Exorcist* was written to persuade those who do not believe that there is a case to be made for the supernatural force of evil in the universe whose game plan is to convice us that he does not exist."

So is the devil for real? The Scriptures and human experience say yes. But Jesus is real too. If our lives are truly and obediently under His Lordship then we have nothing to fear.

So don't let old Slue-Foot frighten you. He may go around "roaring *as* a lion," but the real lion *is* Jesus Christ, the Lion of Judah.

----

* This term more closely reflects that used in the New Testament than does "demon possession." See Frank Longino, "Demonized," *Logos Journal,* vol. 4, no. 1 (1974):19-21.

VII

Hang-Ups and Hang-Overs

Since I have come into the Pentecostal experience, the Lord has led me, through ministering to others, to realize and deal with the many hang-ups and hang-overs that plague people. I define a *hang-up* as an emotional or intellectual obstacle that prevents a Christian from seeking and obtaining the great release of the Pentecostal experience.

One of the biggest hang-ups for Catholics is the question: "Why weren't we ever taught this before by the Church?" The answer is simple. The Church *has always* taught the possibility and the availability of the Spirit-filled life. Throughout the ages the Church has held up the lives of the saints, whose lives abounded with the charismatic gifts, as the model and ideal to be reached by all Christians. So this is not something new; the only thing new about it is that so many people are experiencing it in these days that it has become a movement in the Church.

Another big hang-up is the exercise of the gift of tongues. "Why tongues?" is often the question. "After all, what good is it for me to pray to God in a language I don't understand?"

This was one of my own hang-ups, but when the Lord gave me the gift I realized the tremendous value of praying in

49

tongues. Most of us today pride ourselves on our education; we have high-school diplomas and many of us have had a college education. We think we're pretty intelligent and we can figure out most things that cross our path. To exercise the gift of tongues takes an act of faith and humility. If there is anything that we have to combat within our spirits, it is pride. Praying in tongues, humanly speaking, is a foolish and humiliating act. I believe that in this age of sophistication the Lord uses the gift of tongues to teach us humility and faith, and the rewards are fantastic. I do not believe that there is a greater feeling of release and dependency upon the Lord than when we surrender our understanding and vocal abilities to His use. It is one of the "foolish" things we can do for Jesus that brings great benefit and fruit to our spiritual lives.

Another hang-up is the common practice of Pentecostals of raising their arms in prayer and supplication. It seems to be a foolish and unnecessary exercise—but when we analyze this act, we can see that it is merely an outward expression of inner surrender. We are, after all, creatures of *body*, soul, and spirit, and raising the arms in prayer is an act symbolic of giving our bodies over to the Lord. Paul tells us that our bodies are "temples of the Holy Spirit," so why not let our bodies join our spirit in worship and prayer?

Whatever our own particular hang-up, all we have to do is to ask the Lord in faith to take it away, and He will. "Ask and you shall receive, seek and you shall find."

I define a *hang-over* as an emotional or intellectual prejudice based upon religious tradition, which, while not preventive of the Pentecostal experience, does hang over into the Christian's life even after he has received the baptism in the Holy Spirit, limiting the full extension of his freedom in the Spirit-filled life.

One evening I was invited to speak about the Catholic Pentecostal movement at a Baptist church. After the talk I was stopped by a Protestant lady who insisted on informing me that

50

she used to be a Catholic but had left all that bunk and mumbo jumbo when she found the Lord. She further gloated over the fact that her sister had married an ex-priest. It was a shame, but because of her hang-over, she couldn't really rejoice in what the Lord was doing for so many of her Christian brothers and sisters in the Catholic church. She had reasoned, illogically, that any Catholic who has the Pentecostal experience must leave the Church. This prejudice prevented her from the joy that should have been hers in the fulfillment of the prophecy of Joel, "That in the last days, I will pour out my Spirit upon *all* flesh."

Another example came to my attention one Sunday evening when I was invited to attend a local Pentecostal church. My invitation came from two teen-age boys who belonged to that church but who had been coming to our Catholic Pentecostal meetings. Before I could join the people in prayer, the pastor put me through the third degree. He just couldn't understand how Catholics were receiving the baptism in the Holy Spirit, because, he said, "The Holy Spirit cannot fill an unclean vessel!" Unfortunately, to his mind, if you receive the baptism in the Holy Spirit you just can't remain a Catholic. After all, Catholics have bishops, sacraments, and all those other superstitious and unscriptural things. His particular hang-over prevented him from rejoicing in what the Lord was doing in the Catholic church. He failed to see that the Lord *meets us where we are*.

I could mention many other hang-ups and hang-overs, but the principle of what I am saying here is that we must be completely open to what the Lord is doing, for the Holy Spirit blows where He wills. We must not constrain Him or His action to our own pet theologies or doctrines. If we do, we will miss much of what He has for us. In Revelation the Lord declares, "Behold, I am doing a *new* thing." Let us set aside our prejudices, our hang-ups and hang-overs, and praise the Lord for what He is doing.

51

VIII

The "Cost" in Pentecost

The icy rain slashed against my study window. I was slouched in the familiar cushions of my chair, and my mood matched the foreboding wintry night.

In the three exciting years since I had been baptized in the Holy Spirit, the Lord had allowed me to see victory after victory in my preaching and in my ministry. But something was happening at the same time that was causing a feeling of distressful uneasiness—too many people were flocking to hear Father Orsini, too many were eager to be prayed over by Father Orsini. I was being touted as a healer, a prophet, a miracle worker, and the Jesus whom I loved seemed almost an afterthought in the minds of those desperate people who gathered to see and touch me. I knew it wasn't deliberate on the part of those enthusiastic throngs of souls. I also knew that it was dangerous, since both they and I could be easily led astray by a ministry that claimed to be full-gospel, but shied away from the discipleship of brokenness and suffering. In spite of my public image, I was often overcome with weariness from my constant contact with sickness, hopelessness and demon power.

I knew I was not up to the task. And it was precisely at those times of weariness and weakness when the Lord's mighty power would break through. But again and again, Satan took advantage of my lack of experience and prideful nature. Under the pressure of tasks too great for me, I found myself becoming hypercritical. I began nagging my associates and spent less and less time in prayer.

I begged the Lord to change things so I would learn, truly learn, the wisdom of Saint Paul's request for prayer, "lest preaching to others, I too become a castaway." And the Lord answered that prayer. Immediately. Strikingly. Amply. The next day.

I was on official leave of absence from my diocese. A recent letter from my diocesan office indicated that my request for a year's extension would probably be granted, but there had to be an interview first. I drove the ninety miles to the diocesan office from my home, and when I arrived, the required interview took only an hour.

My requested leave of absence was extended until June 1. But I was informed that newly instituted diocesan policy deprived me of the right to exercise the priestly ministry while I was on leave.

The significance of the policy didn't hit me until I was driving back up the bleak New Jersey Turnpike toward home. Suddenly I realized that for the next five months, I would not be allowed to celebrate Mass publicly, to hear confessions, or to minister in any way. At a stroke, all my public ministry had come to a dead halt. No more prayer meetings, no more speaking engagements—nothing.

When I realized this, I was tempted to rebel in some way. There were many ways to do so. I could defy regulations and continue to minister in secret. If pressure from my superiors became too intense, I could even leave the church and minister in some other denomination. But the Lord witnessed to my spirit, *submit, obey, and be still*. And thus in the midst of a growing ministry, I withdrew. Not willingly, at first, but I knew I had to obey—or all that I had preached, all to which I had given witness, would be destroyed.

I write this to share with my Christian brothers and sisters the difficult and deep lessons the Lord taught me from that February day to the present. I pray that these pages will help all who read them to learn what I have learned and to see what I have seen, in the lively hope that the *full* gospel of Jesus may be taken to their bosom.

IX

Watch Out for the Thorns!

All that I had experienced and much of what I had heard and read in the charismatic renewal had been joy, joy, joy! Alleluia and glory!

No one told me to watch out for the thorns. But thorns there were, plenty of them, and they hurt.

The path *to* Pentecost is laden with thorns and sharp stones—the desperate searching, the wounds and scars of less than perfect human relationships, the disappointments of institutional Christianity, sin, and self-seeking. Although it is undeniably true that Pentecost is a mountaintop experience transfiguring and transforming the soul by the power of the Holy Spirit, the Christian cannot stay on top of the mountain in gilded tabernacles. He must descend, willingly or not, back into the valley of earthly reality.

Just as the path *to* Pentecost is laden with thorns, so is the path *from* Pentecost, but with this tremendous difference: Now the Holy Spirit is released in His fullness, and there is locomotive power on the pathway. Pentecost is the empowering of the Christian to live in the valley, to live out his dying to self, day by day, hour by hour, inch by painful inch.

When I arrived home that memorable February day, I moved slowly from my car to the little path leading to my front door. I observed the rose bushes along the path and clearly saw the dried-up rose hips, deep purple in color, rock hard in texture. Only a few months before, they had been glorious and fiery in splendor, bursting with delightful fragrance. The leafless bushes now showed, in stark relief, the ugly, sharp thorns previously hidden by green foliage.

"How much like my own experiences these past few years," I thought. What spiritual delights, what beauty, what joy, what victory had been mine! But now I was faced with the reality that I was about to enter a secret place filled with private pain. The awesome glory of Mount Tabor would now be balanced by the awesome loneliness of the Mount of Olives. I sensed that Jesus, ever the Master, the Teacher, would lovingly teach me that there are no worthwhile roses without thorns.

As I stepped into the warmth and familiarity of my home, my ears were greeted by the comforting sounds of my mother preparing the evening meal in the kitchen. I slipped into the living room, tears of disappointment and hurt already staining my face. I wanted time to control my emotions so I wouldn't distress my mother with something she couldn't understand.

It was a futile attempt. Mama came into the living room and looked at me intently. With that innate sensitivity of an Italian mother, she knew immediately that something was wrong. Then she sat down in a chair, and I moved over and knelt at her knees. Lovingly, she pressed my head against her bosom. Not a word passed between us, but she sighed deeply and began to weep for my pain. She didn't have to understand the circumstances surrounding the hurt in my heart. She knew with her spirit that her little boy was suffering, and slowly, just as her strength had made me grow in her womb so many years ago, now her strength again flowed into my weakness and absorbed my pain and frustration.

In those moments, the Lord Jesus taught me about His own mother.

In the evangelical and fundamental circles to which much of my ministry had been directed, the question most repeatedly thrown at me was, "Now that you have had the born-again experience and the Baptism in the Holy Spirit, how can you reconcile the Roman Catholic tradition concerning the Virgin Mary?" I had often used an answer attributed to the great Pentecostalist, David du Plessis: "The last recorded words of the Virgin Mary in the New Testament come from the incident at Cana, when she said, 'Do whatever He tells you.' Thus my devotion and veneration for Mary stems from her apparent role in the Scriptures—to direct us to obedience to Jesus, her Divine Son."

While I was on my knees that day, the Lord taught me that while du Plessis' answer was a pretty good one, it wasn't complete. The Catholic Christian devotion to Mary has been more cultural and human than theological and scriptural. The Mediterranean soil and atmosphere of the first Christian missionary effort, the Mediterranean tradition of veneration for the mystery of natural motherhood, was the source of the veneration and devotion to the supernatural motherhood of Mary.

Jesus brought to my mind the beautiful and deep relationship between Himself and His Mother; how she was always there, perhaps not understanding completely what her Son was about, but, nevertheless, trusting without question. What an example for all of us in our own personal relationships with Jesus! Although we do not understand completely the ways of God, yet we must trust, confidently and without question.

Oh the wisdom and compassion of our great God! He comes to us in the person of Jesus, through the totally human vehicle of Mary, and Mary through His grace becomes the model for our own deepening relationship with Him. What more human and easily imitated example could He have given us than His own lovely Mother? What son or daughter has not experienced, howbeit imperfect or limited, the total trust and love of a mother? No longer would I be afraid to declare my love and veneration for Mary, as I have never been afraid to declare the virtues and unselfish love of my own mother.

Thorns are a little price to pay for such beautiful roses.

My mother knew instinctively that no matter what pain and trauma I had endured earlier that day, her mother's arms and heart had begun the healing process within me.

Later that evening, I had to telephone my pastor, Father DelMonte, to inform him that I would no longer be able to assist him at the parish in celebrating the Lord's Supper and the other sacraments. He was distressed, of course, but he counseled obedience to the directives. His wisdom and experience became bulwarks against imprudent action on my part in the months that lay ahead.

As I prepared for bed that evening, I prayed that the Lord would strengthen my resolve to be obedient and submissive to authority, even if it meant total isolation.

x

The Blessing of Misunderstanding

Early the next morning, I arose to celebrate the Lord's Supper privately for myself and my mother. It was a time of great blessing and comfort as we prayed together. The Lord seemed to say, *Don't fret! I have much to teach you. Trust Me!*

After breakfast, I began to contact all who would be affected by my withdrawal from public ministry. First I telephoned my brother in the Lord, Dan Malachuk of Logos International. Dan didn't quite understand the full significance of the new diocesan policy, but he promised prayer and support.

The rest of the day I dictated letters to my unofficial secretary, Florence Vayda. Florence, a faithful member of our Catholic charismatic prayer community in Bayonne, seemed to have received the gift of tears. They always flowed abundantly at our meetings, in prayer, while she listened to Bible teachings. This day her tears stained all of the correspondence necessary for canceling speaking engagements that had been set up all over the country.

That evening, I called an emergency meeting of the pastoral team of the Bayonne charismatic community. At about eight o'clock, we gathered in the rectory of the Assumption Church.

The first to arrive was Brother Dominick Riccio. Brother Rick, as we all called him, rushed in with his usual dynamic enthusiasm and embraced me in his effusive brotherly fashion. When I caught my breath, I saw that Brother Carmen DeLucia was next in line for a bear hug. Brother Carmen, true to form, blurted out, "Okay! What's this all about?" Father Del Monte joined us, and we found ourselves waiting—as usual—for Brother Ken Eliott, the only non-Catholic member of our pastoral team. We often joked that he'd probably be late for the Second Coming. But we understood that Ken often worked late. Finally, he rumbled apologetically through the door, and the meeting began.

I explained as best I could what the situation was, and after the initial shock, accompanied by shouts—very human ones—of disappointment and recrimination, we settled down to pray and ask the Lord's guidance for the future of our prayer community. After some quiet time, I explained that we had to choose one of them to take over my position of leadership. The choice fell on Brother Rick.

I remember thinking to myself, "Poor fellow, now he's going to find out it isn't all glory. He'll have to be here early to set up the chairs, the book table, and see that all is ready. Members of the community will come to him with their petty gripes and complaints. If anything goes wrong, he'll have to bear the brunt of the responsibility." I didn't envy him at all.

We ended with a decision to announce at the prayer meeting scheduled for the next day that I would no longer be in attendance at our prayer meetings because I had been called back to my diocese. It wasn't exactly a deception, yet it wasn't the truth, either. We should have had enough faith in the Lord and in our brothers and sisters to tell them the whole truth. We closed with an uneasy prayer, and sorrowfully took leave of one another.

I walked over to the church to spend some time in prayer in

the presence of Our Lord in the Blessed Eucharist. It seemed to my lively imagination that the Lord began to remonstrate with me: *Why did you allow them to make that decision? And why this long face? Why allow them to feel that you are being unjustly persecuted? Do you enjoy being revered as a martyr? Joseph, Joseph! You know within yourself that you resent authority, and that does not come from My Holy Spirit.*

"But Lord!" I bleated like a lost sheep, "but Lord, I'm only human!"

You're telling Me! I created you, remember? And I recreated you, too. Your ecclesiastical superiors are not acting on whim or out of vengeance. They have nothing against you personally. Don't make this something more than it is.

I was still for a moment, looked around the darkened church, and riveted my attention on the Tabernacle again. After a few moments, I began to pour my heart out:

"Lord, I know that this is an indirect result of my book being published without prior approval. A subtle attitude of disobedience to Church authority seeped through some of the last chapters. I regret that part of my book. I really do. You know I attempted to prevent it being published."

A very feeble attempt, wasn't it, Joe?

"But I did try, Lord, I did! And what about the hundreds of letters I received from ex-Catholics and falling-away priests who testified that they came back to the Church and the ministry because of my book?"

That's beside the point. Yes, I have used the instrument of your book to touch some of My lost sheep and shepherds. Nevertheless, aren't you forgetting that it was you who asked Me to change things so you would learn the wisdom of My apostle Paul's plea, "Lest preaching to others, I too become a castaway"?

"Yes, Lord."

Then be a good student and listen while I teach!

"Yes, Lord."

I slipped away from the church and drove to my sister's house. It was almost midnight, but after that lambasting, I needed some of her coffee and solid faith.

Evelyn was always astounding me with her unquestioning faith in the Lord. She attended our prayer meetings, and I had prayed for her to receive the baptism in the Holy Spirit with the manifestation of praying in tongues. Her faith was a great deal stronger than mine. I knew, for example, that although her son, Frank, had been seriously ill many times, she had never given up. She simply believed, and through the Lord's grace, her faith literally prayed him back to health, time and time again. Evelyn amazed me that night, too. Her coffee was delicious, and her solid faith in the Lord against all odds was highly contagious. I was strengthened just by being in her company.

By the time I dropped into my bed, it was early morning, but sleep would not come. I tossed and turned, my mind churning with thoughts:

"Consider the blessing that misunderstanding will bring when through it you learn to recognize no hand but the faithful hand of your loving Father in heaven. You are giving far too much glory to the devil, the world, and the flesh, in the circumstances of you life. You blame your real or imagined enemies when you are in trouble, but great peace and quietness of heart will be yours when you refuse to recognize second causes in your life. God has been pleased to allow this to happen to you, and your part is to believe that 'all things work together for good to them that love God, to them who are the called according to his purpose' (Rom. 8:28 KJV).

"You find yourself in perplexity over being misunderstood. Rejoice in this blessing, as God is owning you as His son and preparing you for the comfort and blessing of others in the same trial of faith with the same comfort wherewith you yourself will

64

be comforted of God (II Cor. 1:3-4). He is gracing your life with the glorious privilege of sharing in the most intimate sufferings of Christ (Phil. 3:10).

"Through misunderstanding, you will learn that the strength and grace of the Lord can be worked in your life only in the blessing of weakness brought to pass by the thorn in the flesh (II Cor. 12:7).

"The pain that you now experience will be transformed, by grace, into the goodness of God. Thus, like the trampled flower whose perfume rises to bless the foot that crushed it, so your own heart will find no bitterness, seek no revenge, wish no ill. The fullness of your own cup must overflow and bless those who misunderstand you."

A wave of great peace came over me as I began to praise the Lord in other tongues as the Spirit gave utterance, and at last I drifted off into untroubled slumber.

XI

Darkness before Dawn

In that pleasant state between sleeping and waking, I was aware of a distant ringing. Over and over, louder and louder it became, until my mother's voice calling loudly, "Joe!" woke me with a start, and I realized the telephone was ringing. I hopped out of the pleasing warmth of my bed, and scrambled to the phone. Wondering who it could be, I picked up the phone and heard, "Joe, this is Father Del Monte. Could you come down to the rectory to see me right away?"

"Sure, Dom, what's it all about?"

"I can't talk now, just come down."

"Okay. I'll be there in about twenty minutes."

I dressed hurriedly and drove to the rectory. Father Del Monte greeted me and quickly got to the point:

"I just had a call from a monsignor at the Chancery Office. He informed me that the Pentecostal prayer meetings we've been having for the past two years have to be stopped because no permission was ever sought or granted to have them in the first place."

I was stunned. I could hardly believe what I had heard. I looked at Father Del Monte and saw tears forming in his eyes.

After a few moments, I found my voice:

"Dom, what are we going to do?"

"What can we do? We must obey. Let's call Rick to let him know, so when the people come for the prayer meeting tonight, he can tell them."

Brother Rick's reaction was stunned silence. He asked if he could call the monsignor to clarify the directive, and we agreed that would be all right. Half an hour later, he called back and informed us that Father Del Monte had understood the monsignor, all right. The meetings were to be stopped at once.

Rick agreed that we must obey, even if we didn't understand. That night, he met with the large group of people who had come for the prayer meeting and told them that the prayer meetings were being suspended until further notice.

A month later, we were informed that the directive had come as a result of a misunderstanding of diocesan policy, and that we could resume the meetings. During that month, the Lord showed us that all had not been well within our charismatic community. We found dissension, factions, and an underlying current of theological opinion inimical to the Catholic church.

Because of serious doctrinal differences, two members of the pastoral team left, taking with them many members. When the community came together again, the full burden of pastoral leadership rested upon Brother Rick's shoulders, and in the course of a few months, the Bayonne charismatic community ceased to be. And in the deep darkness of the time before dawn, we began to learn some very important lessons.

One apparent lesson was that in any small charismatic group, deep foundations must be laid both in the Word of God *and* in the institutional Church. A ship cast off from its mooring soon drifts away aimlessly and becomes subject to the danger of foundering upon hidden rocks. Natural enthusiasm fanned by supernatural experience can lead only to dangerous postures unless it is tempered by a thorough grounding in the Word of God and a strong link to the body of the institutional Church and to its invaluable experience. The Holy Spirit of God leads us not to fragmentation, but to unity with and in the Body of Christ.

We see in the Old Testament that even though the people of Israel consistently broke their covenant with Yahweh, God did not leave them in order to go and form another people. Rather, He cajoled, He shook, He punished, *He* kept the covenant. So in the New Covenant, inconsistent though His people may be, He does not leave them in their sin; rather, He cajoles, He shakes, He punishes—until they are transformed by the Holy Spirit into a people after His own heart.

The Lord God is infinitely patient in His mercy and His love. It is we, with our individual interpretations of His will, who separate from one another and claim God is "on our side."

I discovered from my own experience how easily one can convince oneself that he is right and everyone else is right or wrong, depending on whether he comes into line with our chosen posture. I myself almost became a victim of the alluring trap of personal cultism. If one is gifted with a "charismatic" personality and preaches a "popular" glory gospel, he has little trouble in building a following. Better still, if he's consistently good enough, an evangelistic association preceded by his name will soon emerge, and finally, if time is on his side, a new denomination will make the scene. What a dreadful waste of energy to build a human temple of transitory glory!

The Lord in His wisdom and love acted swiftly to save me from myself, and in the process taught me that the charismatic renewal is exactly that—a *re*newal of a dimension that has always existed in the Church of Jesus. Revivals, movements, and renewals have come and gone, but the Church of Jesus has always remained—because the Son of the living God is the chief cornerstone.

The Lord taught me that His *full* gospel must be taught and lived; if any *one* facet is emphasized to the detriment of the rest, then the wonderful balance of His life-giving message is thrown off-center. The situation has a parallel in the laws of nutrition. If one consistently emphasizes one element to the neglect of the other elements, the body will eventually suffer disease. I am an active participant in the charismatic renewal—I love what the Lord is doing through it—but He has taught me that the baptism in the Holy Spirit is only one part of His *whole* Gospel. It can be the starting point for many, as it was for me, but one cannot expect to win a race if he runs in place at the starting point and refuses to move down the track.

During the months that followed the cessation of the prayer meetings, my personal prayer life deepened, and the Lord led me out of the darkness of circumstances into the dawning light of His countenance.

XII

What's So Good About Suffering?

March was cold, blustery, rainy. The rain was almost maddening, day after day, seemingly without end. It was the kind of weather that makes people draw into themselves. The liturgical season was Lent, and the readings from the Scriptures assigned for the daily Eucharists I was celebrating privately, echoed the somberness of the weather, setting out in detail the sufferings of our Lord as He approached Calvary.

Time lay heavy upon me. After spending a few hours a day in study and writing on my doctoral dissertation, I retired to my room to be alone with the Lord. During this quiet time of withdrawal, I contemplated the role of suffering in the Christian's life.

While it is true that Jesus paid the price for our salvation and we can do nothing to add to what He already paid, it is only fair that we *share* in that price, if we are truly His disciples. The Christian walk is tempered by shadows and rainy days. It has to be, for the life on which sun always shines will become dry and unproductive.

Jesus calls us to come to Him and live, but before we can live that abundant life, we must die to self. It is only when we are dead to self and alive to God that we are truly His disciples. God strives to make us lovable, and the process, a never-ending one in this lifetime, is often painful. In Malachi's prophecy of Christ, we read that He will be like a refiner's fire (Mal. 3:2).

After the initial enthusiasm of the Pentecostal experience with its ecstasy and glorious operation of the gifts of the Holy Spirit, Jesus, through His Spirit, calls each of us to a deeper identification with Him through suffering. It is at this point that many draw away in shock and disappointment.

We don't hear too much about pain and suffering in "charismatic" preaching, and that is precisely why the understanding of many charismatic Christians, especially new ones, is out of balance. Calvary's Cross is all right for Jesus, but please don't ask me to get up there, too.

The *whole* Word of God, the *full* gospel, includes the important dimension of identification with Jesus' sufferings (Phil. 3:10). Pain moves men toward God. Consider the example of Job. Pain is an absolute necessity if we are to follow Jesus, because the human spirit refuses to surrender self-will as long as all seems to be going well. There are times when God wants to show us His vision of reality, but He cannot because our field of vision is already filled with our own desires. He wants to give us something, but we are too preoccupied and self-content. Then, at the very moment we think all is well, something happens to shatter our illusion. Pain teaches us that we can endure obedience to God and His appointed ministers.

A word of caution is in order here. By no means are we to look for pain or inflict suffering upon ourselves. God is not served by self-inflicted suffering. Guilt is not washed away by pain, but by the blood of Jesus. Saint John Bosco was criticized by his contemporaries because the rule of the Salesian Society which he founded did not impose self-inflicted penances like the other religious societies of his time. Don Bosco answered

72

that the pain and suffering that God sends into every Christian's life are enough to effect His purpose. All we have to do is to accept, joyfully, what He sends, without trying to second-guess God.

Pain serves no purpose if it makes us bitter or produces a feeling of superiority. Once pain has taught us the lesson that God wants us to learn, and He offers us relief, we must not refuse it on the grounds that we are choosing to follow a "higher way."

There is the kind of suffering to which a few are called which can be explained only in the light of God's eternal providence, as expressed by Saint Paul when he wrote that all things work together for the good of those who love God and are called according to His purpose (Rom. 8:28). Only eternity will reveal the usefulness of some suffering. I am thinking of those precious Christians who are afflicted by either physical or spiritual suffering and whose faith is strong, but who never receive the blessing of healing. Peter tells us, "Beloved, think it not strange concerning the fiery trial which is to try you, as though some strange thing happened unto you: But rejoice, inasmuch as ye are partakers of Christ's sufferings; that, when his glory shall be revealed, you may be glad also with exceeding joy" (I Pet. 4:12-13 KJV).

The history of Christianity shines with those who have suffered with Christ and who in the end were the bearers of victory: "If so be that we suffer with him, that we may be also glorified together" (Rom. 8:17 KJV). These are the blessed ones who, with Paul, had no regrets in belonging to "the fellowship of his sufferings" (Phil. 3:10 KJV).

It is in the hour of suffering for God's sake that the believer shows the most intimate likeness of Christ. The Christian is called to suffer with God and for God. Jesus says to His followers, "You are those who have continued with me in my trials" (Luke 22:28).

There is a fellowship of Christ's suffering to which all are called, but not all enter. It is Christ within us who suffers and is continually persecuted. "If the world hates you, know that it has hated me before it hated you" (John 15:18).

Believers who fellowship in Christ's suffering seem to know Him in a closer, more intimate way. They stand with Him in His agony at Gethsemane. They hunger with Him in the desert and are tempted by Satan. They touch the repulsively ill with Him. They weep with Him over Jerusalem and the world.

I have had the privilege of knowing such a one, of sitting at his feet since childhood. My pastor, Father Dominic Del Monte, has been for me an example of one sharing the fellowship of Christ's suffering. I have seen him crucified over and over again by misunderstanding and neglect, but each time he grows stronger, and his identification with Jesus closer. He is one who has emptied himself for the sheep given him to pastor. In the midst of tribulation and sorrow, his face shines with the glory of Jesus.

As the dreary days of March hurried toward the promise of April, the rumors concerning my situation began to fly:

"He's been defrocked because of all that crazy Holy Roller stuff!"

"Oh! Father Orsini! Well, I hear that he's left the Church, married a nun, and become a Protestant minister."

As the rumors grew more and more ridiculous, Brother Pancratius, my "God-father," parried the blows. It had fallen to him to substitute for me in many speaking engagements. Poor Brother Panky! He had never imagined that this "God-son" of his would be so troublesome.

The incident that caused me more distress than any other at this time, was that many of the national leadership of the

Catholic charismatic renewal at Notre Dame held me in suspicion because I had never made the pilgrimage to the annual National Conference on the Charismatic Renewal held there. Brother Panky had to be my apologist and explain that I had never attended the Notre Dame conference because it was scheduled at a time when it was impossible for me to attend. He explained, also, that I was a priest in good standing, and the reason for the present silence was simply because I was being obedient to diocesan directives.

However, after some reflection, I realized it wasn't important what anyone thought. All I wanted to do was to follow Jesus as He led.

April came swiftly, and on Easter Sunday, I attended Mass in another city. The Lord comforted me with His presence and a sense of peace.

XIII

With Strings Attached

It was almost time for the end of my leave of absence. Looking forward to the day when I would be exercising the priestly ministry once again, I wrote a letter to my ecclesiastical superiors asking them to consider appointing me to a special apostolate when I returned on June 1. I requested an appointment as Diocesan Coordinator of Catholic Charismatic Groups. Because of my experience in the charismatic renewal, I felt I would be qualified for such a position. I could work full time at the job, overseeing existing groups, starting new ones, writing a weekly article for the diocesan newspaper, and conducting Charismatic Days of Renewal from parish to parish.

I received a considerate reply to the effect that I couldn't be appointed to this kind of position immediately, but that there was a chance for the future. At the end of May, I received my official appointment as associate pastor to Monsignor Michael Argullo at the Church of Saint Paul, Stone Harbor, New Jersey. I was delighted. It was a beautiful assignment, and I would be serving under a pastor whom I greatly admired. I had been his assistant for a summer season a few years earlier and knew Monsignor Mike to be a man of prayer.

Early on the morning of June first, I said goodbye to my mother. Having lived at home for the past two years, it was difficult for me to pack up and leave, especially on my birthday. The ride down to Stone Harbor took almost three hours. When I arrived at Saint Paul's rectory, Monsignor Mike welcomed me with open arms.

I soon became accustomed to the routine of parish life, and I thoroughly enjoyed the warm friendship and support of Monsignor Mike.

He knew a great deal about the Catholic charismatic renewal. He had read my book, and one evening we sat together on the rectory porch after our evening meal and talked about it. Monsignor admitted that although he was not personally attracted to that type of spiritual experience, he saw great value in it. We discussed the possibility of starting a Catholic Pentecostal prayer group for the parish.

For the next few Sundays, I preached about the basic principles of the charismatic renewal. Many came to see me after Mass to ask where they could attend a prayer meeting, so we decided to begin prayer meetings at Saint Paul's. They were an immediate success. The Lord began to bless those who came for the baptism in the Holy Spirit with the evidence of praying in tongues.

Then one day, I received a letter from my diocesan office which was a reply to a request for me to speak about the Catholic Pentecostal movement at an ecumenical gathering. The request was denied, and the letter implied that all such requests would be denied, at least for the immediate future. I accepted this decision without question, and realized I had to go a step further, so I suspended the prayer meetings. It was a simple decision on my part to obey not only the letter of the law, but also the spirit of the law. Everyone concerned accepted and respected my decision and continued to attend already established prayer meetings in distant areas.

During the month of August, I continued my parochial work in earnest and spent much time in prayer. I began to think about the role of obedience to authority in the life of the charismatic Christian, especially obedience to Church authority. I realized from my own experience that obedience is absolutely necessary for the complete peace we seek in knowing the will of God for our lives. As a professing Catholic Christian, it would be incongruous for me to use my Pentecostal experience as a wedge between me and those ordained by God to rule my Church. We are, I believe, called by Jesus to be an example of obedience. We are called to meekness, willingness to be trained for service, and to respond to higher authority.

Jesus calls us not to timidity or self-rule, but to obedience and submission to those He has set up in authority over us. The call to obedience is a shattering one, because the cost of obedience is the cost of dying to self. The daily walk with Jesus is a learning-to-be-made-willing process. Few of us are willing to do all God wants us to do, especially when God's will is made known to us by agents as human as we are. But we must be willing to be made willing. It is sad to see believers rebelling against God just because God chooses to rule His Church through this or that human agent. Jesus has recently become a popular example of a totally free, uninhibited being, and has arisen as the Superstar of liberated unhung-up persons. It must be remembered that He represents the greatest example of servitude.

The charismatic Catholic must be a willing servant of God's Word, and a willing servant of His Church. There can never be a conflict of substance between the two; at the very least, there can be a conflict as to method, as was evidenced in the discussions of Vatican Council II. Jesus left to those who would occupy positions of leadership in His Church some very definite instructions as to how they were to exercise the authority He would give them:

> You know that the rulers of the Gentiles lord it over them, and their great men exercise authority over them. It shall not be so among you; but whoever would be great among you must be your servant, and whoever would be first among you must be your slave; even as the Son of man came not to be served but to serve, and to give his life as a ransom for many. (Matt. 20:25-28)

It may be true that some have abused this authority, but the abuse of authority does not negate its validity. It is not to be rebelliously disregarded, rather it is to be prayed for until it comes in line with the intention of Jesus in its establishment.

God honors our prayers and our sacrifices. But above all, He seeks those who will serve, who will obey. He appreciates our obedience more than all our talent, more than all the astounding charismatic gifts that may grace our lives.

Thousands of Catholics throughout the world are entering into the Pentecostal experience, and they are discovering that this experience comes with strings attached—strings attached to the discipleship of suffering and to obedience to both God's Word and the order that the Church rightly brings into their lives and experiences.

XIV

All Things Work Together for Good

On September 25, I received notification that I was being transferred to the church of Saint Edward in Pine Hill, New Jersey, where I would be associate pastor. By this time, I had already received permission from my superiors to become involved in the charismatic renewal within the confines of the diocese. I was not familiar with the area to which I was being assigned, but I had been forewarned it wouldn't be an easy one for a number of reasons, one of which was that it was an economically depressed area.

The assignment did prove to be difficult. It needed a man with more pastoral leanings than I had. I asked to be put back into full-time high school teaching, because this was what I had been trained for. I had many years of experience, and I loved to teach teenagers. From the end of September until near the end of January when I was assigned as a teacher of religion on the faculty of Gloucester Catholic High School in Gloucester City, New Jersey, I caught a bad case of the Pine Hill blues. It was simply a case of the wrong man for the wrong job—a carpenter just does not feel competent to do a plumber's job. That's the way it was for me. But all things work unto good for those who love God, and this gave me ample time to reflect, to pray, and to study. Much of my time was spent in putting the finishing touches on my dissertation, *An Educational History of the Pentecostal Movement*, and my study led me to meditate upon what Jesus was doing through the charismatic renewal.

God wants us to live in union with Him and with one another through Jesus Christ. We find this revealed in John's Gospel, chapters 14-17. God wants us to enter into that same kind of relationship which He has with Himself. Just as the Trinity is one, so does the Lord want us to be one with Him, the Father, and the Spirit. This is an amazing thing, an incomprehensible, beautiful, and loving fact. The Source of everything wants us to share fully in the life which He has with Himself. This is what man was made for. It is in our unity with God that we become complete. Creation, redemption, and the gift of the Spirit are all things which God has given to man to enable him to live with God. None of these things are ends in themselves, but through them, God and His creature—man—can live together, with man loving his God to his fullest capacity.

Jesus came to heal the breach between God and man and bring us together again in Himself. He is the full revelation of God to man, and in His Spirit alone can we come to union with the Father. It is the Spirit of Jesus which gives us the power to become the sons of God which He wants us to be.

> If a man loves me, he will keep my word, and my Father will love him, and we will come to him and make our home with him. (John 14:23)

We are all called to this union with God; there is no one whom He wishes to exclude. All a man has to do is to open the door to Jesus and keep His commandments, and the Lord will begin to draw that man to Himself and the Father.

In the seventeenth chapter of John's Gospel, Jesus prays to

the Father that we may all be one—perfectly one, just as He and the Father are one. Jesus wants us to be His people. Just as surely as man was made to live in union with God, so too was he made to live in union with his fellowman. God lives in unity, and unity is also the perfect and only way for man to live with man. Jesus says in that same chapter of John that it is our unity with one another that is the greatest witness to Himself (John 17:23). This may sound strange to some people, but it is true. Sometimes people feel that it ought to be the signs and wonders performed by Christians which show the Lord to be truly Lord. But practical experience has proven the truth of the words of Jesus. Many times people come to see a charismatic community and are totally unimpressed by the signs and wonders, the prophecies and speaking in tongues. What has touched them and has led them to seek a deeper life with the Lord has been the love and unity which they have seen and felt among the members of the community. "This is my commandment, that you love one another as I have loved you" (John 15:12).

It is the Lord Jesus Himself who is the source of our love and unity with one another. We cannot love one another unless we have first let the Lord love each one of us. Many people make the mistake of thinking that they have a source of love in their own selves, that they can love another with a love which is their own. This is not true. All love comes from God. A love that hasn't first come from the source of all love is not a true love, a genuine love. Our love comes from Jesus, through us, to each other. Jesus says that He is the vine and we are the branches. The branches can bear nothing unless they are part of the vine. Paul says that Christ is the Head of the body. The body is nothing without the Head. Our love and unity are dependent upon our being grafted into Christ, becoming a part of His body.

In the Acts of the Apostles we find that those who believed

"were of one heart and soul" (4:32) and that they "devoted themselves to the apostles' teaching and fellowship, to the breaking of bread and the prayers" (2:42). And again, that "all who believed were together and had all things in common" (2:44). These were all signs of unity and oneness in the early Church. This is how we begin to live our lives together as Jesus wants us to.

To many people, the early Church is too remote to be anything more than just a nice ideal, *not* something which can exist here and now. Some present-day charismatic communities, however, are experiencing the reality and beauty of community.

Every Christian is called to make total commitment of himself to his Creator and Savior. This step to totally giving oneself over to God is not just something God asks only of those who have reached a plateau of holiness. Commitment to the lordship of Jesus Christ is a basic step for our Christian growth. Surrendering ourselves to Jesus Christ takes an act of one's will, deliberately turning to God, making the decision that says, "I am going to follow Jesus Christ and give my life to Him." Surrendering ourselves to Christ is something we must do every day of our lives.

This commitment to Jesus Christ is the first step for entering into the fullness of life as God's sons. We must be convinced that Jesus Christ is the Way, the Truth, and the Life.

Repentance is a second step. It is a deliberate turning away from sin and evil, the yielding of our human weaknesses and deficiencies to the Lord. Again, we must not fall into the error of viewing repentance as something we do just once. It is a daily act of turning away from sin and giving ourselves over to God.

Saint Paul speaks of repentance as a dying to our old self of sin and rising to the new life of Jesus Christ:

We know that our old self was crucified with him so that

84

the sinful body might be destroyed, and we might no longer be enslaved to sin. For he who has died is freed from sin. But if we have died with Christ, we believe that we shall also live with him. . . . So you also must consider yourselves dead to sin and alive to God in Christ Jesus. (Rom. 6:6-8,11)

On the day of Pentecost, Peter spoke out to the people and instructed them on how they should turn to the Lord:

Repent, and be baptized every one of you in the name of Jesus Christ for the forgiveness of your sins; and you shall receive the gift of the Holy Spirit. (Acts 2:38)

Jesus Christ is the one who frees us from our sins. Jesus Christ is the one who delivers us from whatever bond of oppression or sin holds us back from living more fully in God's life and presence. We cannot free ourselves from self-centeredness and sinfulness. Only God's power and grace can free us. It is the power of God's Spirit which changes us and molds us into the image of Jesus Christ.

We must repent before asking to be baptized into the full life of the Holy Spirit. God's Spirit can fill us and work in us only to the degree that we are open to God and empty of self.

Repentance requires humility. To humble oneself is to admit before God that we are weak and sinful creatures and that we need God's healing power and strength to change us and make us whole in Him. Humility opens us up to receiving God's power for combating and overcoming sin. It opens us up to the Spirit's work of sanctification.

An honest appraisal of ourselves is necessary. We must look at ourselves and see where we are lacking and falling short as true sons of God. It is not enough just to tell God that we are sinful. We must confess before God all our sins. We must renounce evil and the sins of the flesh, the devil, and the world. Until we do so, we will be enslaved to them. Renunciation of sin cannot be complete until we make amends, where possible, for the wrongs we have done before God and men. We must strive to restore what we have taken and damaged by our wrongdoing.

It is not enough that we give up our ways of sin, but we must also forgive others, as God has forgiven us so much, time and time again. Finally, as children of God, we should gladly and unhesitatingly accept the Father's mercy and forgiveness. It is wrong for us to think that God would not forgive us, to fall into self-pity and refuse to consider God's mercy. God is slow to anger and quick to forgive.

These are important truths that God is teaching through the present outpouring of His Holy Spirit. I had ample time to think on them during my time in Pine Hill.

Back to the Vineyard

My new teaching job began on January 29. I had just returned from a pleasant ten-day vacation with my brother Toto and his children in the Caribbean. Refreshed in body and spirit, I arrived at school with a sense of eagerness and anticipation. It was wonderful to be back in the vineyard again, doing what I was meant to do. I was teaching three subjects—Marriage, History of the Reformation, and Eastern Religions.

When I arrived back at the rectory in Pine Hill after my first day of teaching, I was gloriously tired, but with the kind of weariness that felt good. I was back where I belonged.

I didn't tell my students that I was a Catholic Pentecostal, but somehow they discovered it and began to ask me questions after class. I answered them as best I could, giving them a brief overview of the charismatic renewal. I explained that God's incarnation in Jesus clearly demonstrated His interest in the world, in flesh and blood, and everything which belongs to human life. I told them that God does not merely express His opinion about human affairs; rather, He claims dominion over all the things of the world. He commands His disciples to advance to the ends of the earth, and He equips them with special abilities and powers for the mission.

We went on to discuss how God's reality and human involvement are again and again made questionable by Christians' weakness and silence. The world is waiting for proof of God's existence in the lives and actions of those who claim to be His children. And our God, who has proclaimed Himself the Savior of men, proves His reality through the things He does in this world.

Considering the history recorded in the Book of Acts and the Epistles, we saw that God's reality was self-evident to the first Christians. They knew no difference between holiday and everyday, making the first day of the week, then a working day, their special day for worship. They understood their Lord's commission to evangelize the world to mean not only bringing the gospel to unknown lands, but sanctification of all areas of human life. If they met a sick person, they knew that they were called to pray for healing. In their communities, they dealt with the same kinds of problems which are still urgent today—racial integration, emancipation, consideration for the poor. These first-century Christians expected God's power to be seen in all areas of their world. The signs and wonders which accompanied the preaching of the Word were the effects and proofs of God's reality.

I reminded my students that the natural gifts were insufficient for transforming their environment and society. They recognized their own intellectual, physical, and moral weaknesses. But through the Holy Spirit, whom they had received at the beginning of their spiritual life, they knew they were powerfully equipped to be His witnesses.

"Christians today have the same task," I said. "And the power and gifts of the Holy Spirit are still promised *and* received by the disciples of Jesus. Because the problems of our times have grown to overwhelming proportions, we need

God's power to prevent us from perishing in chaos and conflict. For this reason, He has sent us the charismatic renewal, so that Christians can express in their lives the reality of Jesus."

This was not exactly the kind of answer for which my students were looking. They wanted to hear about all the "neat stuff," like speaking in other languages and healing. I tried to explain to them that these dramatic spiritual "fireworks" were only a part of the total reality of what God was doing in the charismatic renewal. I promised them that, in due time, we would discover together what it all meant, and they would hear about all the "neat stuff," too.

During the months that followed, I taught all the subject matter prescribed in the curriculum and the Lord also provided time necessary to give my students a thorough grounding and catechesis on the person and work of the Holy Spirit. Students came to recognize the action of the Spirit at work in the lives of men throughout the history of mankind. In the Old Testament, the Spirit worked through a few specific individuals appointed by God to be prophets, kings, rulers, judges, etc. In the New Testament, in the Acts of the Apostles, we saw the Spirit at work in the lives of all Christians, men and women, young and old. This outpouring of the Spirit on all men fulfilled Joel's prophecy:

> And it shall come to pass afterward, that I will pour out my spirit on all flesh; your sons and your daughters shall prophesy, your old men shall dream dreams, and your young men shall see visions. Even upon the menservants and maidservants in those days, I will pour out my spirit. (Joel 2: 28-29)

In several places in Acts are recorded instances of the apostles laying on hands for the imparting of the Holy Spirit: Peter and John at Samaria—Acts 8:14-17; Paul at

Ephesus—Acts 19:1-7. Paul wrote to the Corinthians:

> To each is given the manifestation of the Spirit for the common good. . . . For by one Spirit we were all baptized into one body—Jews or Greeks, slaves or free—and all were made to drink of one Spirit. (I Cor. 12:7, 13)

Jesus Christ had promised the apostles that He would send the Holy Spirit to them. Until Christ's redemption had been won for all men, the Spirit could not be poured out on all mankind. It was only after Jesus' death and resurrection that the salvation of men had been accomplished and the promise of the Spirit's outpouring could be fulfilled.

This outpouring of God's Spirit was meant for all men who would believe in Jesus Christ, not just in the early Christian communities, but for the Church for all time. We can see the action and power of the Spirit in the lives of many saints throughout the centuries. Saint Francis of Assisi, Saint Catherine of Siena, and Saint Vincent Ferrer are among the notable charismatic saints.

Today, more than in any other time in history, there is an urgent need for the renewal of the power and action of the Spirit as at the first Pentecost. The Vatican Council was a summons for a renewal in the life of the Church. Pope John XXIII prayed that the Holy Spirit would pour out His works upon the whole Church as at the first Pentecost:

> May there be repeated thus in the Christian families the spectacle of the apostles gathered together in Jerusalem after the Ascension of Jesus to heaven, when the newborn Church was completely united in communion of thought and prayer with Peter and around Peter, the shepherd of the lambs and of the sheep. And may the Divine Spirit deign to answer in a most comforting manner the prayer that rises daily to Him from

every corner of the earth: "Renew your wonders in our time, as though for a new Pentecost, and grant that the holy Church, preserving unanimous and continuous prayer, together with Mary the mother of Jesus, and also under the guidance of St. Peter, may increase the reign of the Divine Saviour, the reign of truth and justice, the reign of love and peace. *Amen*.

Pope John, Humanae Salutis

The charismatic renewal of the Spirit within the Catholic Church in the United States began in 1967. Since then, the Pentecostal experience of the gifts and fruits of the Spirit has spread among Catholics all across the United States and Canada and all around the world.

Jesus Christ is the one who baptizes us with the Spirit. When we pray with people and lay hands on them for the baptism in the Spirit, we are making intercession to God for them, asking that Jesus Christ baptize them with His Spirit.

This baptism in the Spirit is not an isolated experience, an end in itself. The baptism is an initiation into the full life of the Spirit. It is the beginning of a totally new relationship with the Holy Spirit, the start of a new way of growing with the power of God, as our life begins to be reoriented and empowered by God's Spirit.

By viewing the baptism in the Spirit within the context of the much larger picture, the total Christian life, we avoid picturing God's power as something static or something one just "gets" and "possesses." We see the power of God's Spirit as a dynamic force that works through time to change and transform an individual and a community more and more into the likeness of Christ.

The role of faith cannot be underestimated. It is the essential requirement to receiving the baptism and the gifts. Faith is a stepping out for God. The Gospel account of Peter stepping out

91

of the boat onto the water is an excellent example of this kind of faith. We cannot sit back and wait for God to hit us on the head with the baptism in the Spirit. We have to put our faith into action and expect God to give us the Spirit.

Our faith is based on the promises of God's words. In praying for the baptism in the Spirit, we claim Christ's promise, "How much more will the heavenly Father give the Holy Spirit to those who ask him" (Luke 11:13).

The Spirit wants to work in and through us and wants to give us His gifts for the building up of the Christian community, for strengthening the individual, and for equipping us for the various works God calls us to do:

> And his gifts were that some should be apostles, some prophets, some evangelists, some pastors and teachers, for the equipment of the saints, for the work of ministry, for building up the body of Christ, until we all attain to the unity of the faith and of the knowledge of the Son of God, to mature manhood, to the measure of the stature of the fulness of Christ. (Eph. 4:11-13)

A first step to receiving the gifts is having a desire for them. Saint Paul says: "Make love your aim, and earnestly desire the spiritual gifts" (I Cor. 14:1). God gives these gifts freely to whomever He chooses. He chooses those who are open and receptive to the working of God's Spirit.

Tongues is an important gift for the person seeking to enter into the full life of the Spirit. Paul instructs the Corinthians, "Now I want you all to speak in tongues" (I Cor. 14:5). The gift of tongues has a real value and importance for our growth as Christians. One important aspect of tongues is that it is a gift of prayer and a gift of praise. Every Christian needs to learn how to pray more effectively and more deeply. The gift of tongues can deepen a person's prayer life. Tongues can teach a person how to praise God. It is the Spirit within us, praising God perfectly. The Spirit also intercedes for us through this gift, praying to the Father for our needs and the needs of others, hidden even from ourselves (Rom. 8:26-27).

Praying in tongues is a means of growing closer to Christ. It is a gift we all need to have right from the start of our new entrance into the full life God's Spirit. We should with real confidence claim this gift at our baptism in the Spirit. We do not need to wait for this gift or shy away from it because of our unworthiness. It is a gift God gives freely, simply because we ask for it. It is not necessary that a person "psych himself up" or feel emotionally ready for receiving this gift. Three things are basically required: First, we should desire this gift; we should hunger and thirst for whatever God wants to give us. Second, we should ask in *faith* for this gift. Faith is based on the promise of Christ that He would give us the power of His Spirit. Third, we, ourselves, must cooperate with God by *speaking out* in faith and expecting God to give us the utterance.

There are some people who come seeking the baptism who say that they don't want the gift of tongues. This is a wrong attitude arising mostly from their fear of making a fool of themselves by babbling incoherently. They are placing restrictions on God and His working; they are not really being open as God wants them to be. God wants to give these people the gift of His Spirit, but He wants them to accept Him on His own terms, completely and openly willing to receive any gift He wants to give them.

The lessons learned in receiving the gift of tongues can be applied to all the gifts of the Spirit. We must yield to the Spirit and cooperate with God. God's Spirit will not work within us unless we allow ourselves to become His instruments. We have to use our bodies and our faculties in cooperation with the Spirit's manifestations of power.

XVI

Eat All Your Spinach, Or You Won't Grow Up Big and Strong!

The months of March and April slipped by rapidly. I was totally involved in preparing classes, marking papers and tests, counseling students, and studying for the oral defense of my dissertation that would take place in May. By the time I arrived back at the rectory each day, the sun had already set. In the midst of all this flurry of activity, I often noticed that my spiritual batteries were wound down almost to the point of exhaustion. But there was always an evening's conversation with Father John Frey, the young priest who had taken my place as associate pastor, and this was usually enough to perk me up for the next day. Out of all possible priests the Lord could send to Pine Hill to take my place, Father John was really a gift from heaven. Not only was his disposition one of calm assurance, but he was also a participant in the charismatic renewal.

A great spiritual uplifting was provided once each month when I participated in a concelebrated Eucharistic liturgy with my brothers and sisters of the Camden Catholic charismatic community which met each week at the Church of St. Rose of Lima in Haddon Heights, New Jersey.

Dr. Frank Iula was the diminutive but dynamic leader of the Camden charismatic group. I had known Dr. Frank from the very beginning of my priestly ministry, as he was my physician. Now, through the baptism in the Holy Spirit, he and his wife Rose had become spiritual physicians as well, not only for me, but for the hundreds who came to the prayer meetings each week. Through our ministry to one another and to others, we learned the spiritual application of a common admonition we had all heard as children, "Eat all your spinach, or you won't grow up big and strong!" What our parents were telling us, in effect, was that although spinach seemed to be unappealing and unappetizing, the nutrients it contained were so beneficial to our growth and health, we should discipline ourselves to make it a regular part of our diet.

In the spiritual realm, the Pentecostal experience, the baptism in the Holy Spirit, could be compared to the popular foods—pizza and hot dogs. Everybody likes pizza and hot dogs, but you can't make a steady diet of them and stay healthy. Other less popular foods, like liver and spinach, must be included for a balanced diet. So in the things of the Spirit, there must be a variety of elements to insure growth and maturation. The Pentecostal experience is the first thing on the spiritual menu, but what follows are equally important experiences to insure the proper balance of a healthy Christian life.

For many, the period following the reception of the baptism of the Spirit contains a whole gamut of reactions and emotions, the result of a spiritual experience which leaves the person freer and happier than he has ever felt before. Next there may be the I-hope-it-lasts reaction, resulting from crowding doubts and fears that the Holy Spirit may be taken away if one isn't careful. Last, and most common, is a feeling of disappointment because the gift of tongues or some other gift has not yet been received. This disappointment does not necessarily mean a lessening of faith, but someone more mature in the life of the

Spirit should take time to explain these things to the newly Spirit-filled Christians and to pray with them.

Each of those reactions must be dealt with tenderly and lovingly. Each newly baptized-in-the-Spirit Christian must be convinced that the "veteran" really understands what he is going through and be willing to talk and pray about it with him. This can be the special ministry of some who have been baptized in the Spirit and are committed members of the community—sort of a spiritual "buddy" system. The counselor must be careful not to squash the euphoria of anyone, nor demand more than anyone is able to give, nor brush off as unimportant or ridiculous the disappointment or doubts of anyone. God leads each one who is newly baptized in the Spirit, and the charismatic community's responsibility is to understand and aid that leading. Christian fellowship is the means through which the Lord leads these little ones to a closer relationship with Himself. There may be some "veterans" in the community who don't feel equal to the task. They should be reminded that if they are begging off because they discern a lack of maturity and wisdom in their own Christian experience, they should pray.

> If any of you lacks wisdom, let him ask God, who gives to all men generously and without reproaching, and it will be given him. But let him ask in faith. (James 1:5-6)

Both seekers and new recipients of the Pentecostal experience must be given a *realistic* and encouraging picture of what it means to grow in the Christian life. The Christian life is a life of balance and dedication to a deepening relationship with Jesus and other Christians. Dedication is important, for without it, the means of growth are of little value. It is for this reason, and from my own observation, that I have serious reservations concerning an indiscriminate ministry of the

Pentecostal reality to teens and pre-teens. From what I have observed firsthand, it is only the exceptionally mature youngster who is capable of the necessary dedication indispensable for growth in the Spirit.

I have found many confused about what growth in the Christian life is all about. Many have been trained in a certain type of spirituality which says that being a better or stronger Christian depends on how much one does of or by himself. Many look at the great and popular Catholic saints as people who gave up many things and spent long hours in prayer and penance. Thus, the whole process of Christian growth has been conceived in quantitative terms—if you wanted to be holy, you had to do more for a longer period of time. But this is not the type of growth that was really taking place. It just looked that way to people who didn't understand what a particular saint was really doing. What was actually happening was a slow transformation *within* the saint—a death to self and a coming alive to Christ.

It is this death to self we have to undergo in order to become like Jesus. We must die to sin and to anything not seen in the person of Christ. It takes a lot of time and patience to become the person Christ wants us to be. The saints that the Church holds up to us as examples of what we also can become, didn't arrive at sainthood overnight. They sought the Lord every day and waited on Him *patiently*, because they knew it was Jesus who gave the growth and not something they did. Jesus leads each one of us at his own speed. He expects our *perseverance*, *patience*, and *trust*. A transformation is a hidden thing, and just because we can't see ourselves growing every day, it doesn't mean that growth isn't happening. We couldn't see the immediate results of physical growth from our eating that unpleasant spinach, but we did grow.

There are four elements necessary to the growth of a Christian. This has been borne out by the practical experiences

98

of many in the charismatic renewal.

The first element is prayer. There is an absolute necessity to speak to God every day in prayer and allow Him to speak to us. This is how we come to know Jesus and the Father through the Holy Spirit. If we love someone, we want to know them in a more intimate way, and we naturally spend more time with that person. To say that we love God, especially after we have received the awesome blessing of the Pentecostal experience, and not spend time with Him in intimate communion, except at prayer meetings, is to say that our love is lukewarm. Love and communication must grow every day, and so we must spend time with Him every day.

Another element is study. One of the things which seem to come universally to people as a result of Holy Spirit baptism is the desire to spend more time reading Scripture. This should be encouraged. God desires to reveal Himself to us through Scripture, and we should open the door for this avenue of revelation. God desires that we know Him fully and completely.

Some people have the problem of not knowing how to read the Scriptures. As the Scriptures came about by men prayerfully and faithfully recording what God had shown Himself to be, they should be read in the same spirit, *prayerfully* and *faithfully*. Commentaries may or may not be helpful, according to the natural intellectual abilities of the readers. Other books may be helpful also, especially those spiritual classics in the treasury of the Church's experience, and a discriminating choice of works by authors now involved in the charismatic renewal.

Another very important element in Christian growth is Christian action. The Pentecostal movement has been criticized because many of its participants seem to be inactive in important social questions. No one person can solve the problems of hunger, poverty, racism, war, and urbanization single-handedly and in one day. But neither will the problems begin to be alleviated unless the followers of Christ in this world seek out how to best accomplish the will of God in these areas. Our charismatic experiences do not absolve us from becoming involved. On the contrary, we have received the power to be witnesses to Christ and are thus given the tools to effect real and lasting change. A refusal to get involved in these crucial areas is a refusal to grow.

The actions we undertake should always be founded in prayer and in full accord with the will of the Lord. There are many committees and groups clamoring to get something done, but we must carefully seek God's guidance before joining them. The best way to approach the possibilities for renewing the temporal order is from the standpoint of the whole community. The whole community should support the activities of its members with prayer, active help, or encouragement. Any project which is from the Lord will find the strength and support of the whole Church community. Because Jesus has given us His Spirit, Christians have the power to transform the world for Christ.

The final essential element for Christian growth is community. In my experience, community or fellowship is one of the finest elements for encouraging Christian growth, because it is practical and down-to-earth. Charismatic prayer communities differ from place to place, but there are elements common and applicable to all. The way to become fully part of a community is to agree to have that special love and concern for one another which the Lord wills in the community. This takes definite commitment to attend the functions of a particular community. A person can hardly expect to be a loving and intimate member of a community if he is never around. I have seen many charismatic communities thrown into confusion by a lack of loving concern on the part of the members for one another.

People become integrated members of the community by submitting themselves to the discipline of the community. A community without discipline is not a community at all and probably won't hold together very long. If a person refuses to submit himself to the discipline of the community, then he ceases to grow as a member. The same thing is true in the relationship of the charismatic communities with the wider community of the institutional Church. Discipline within and by the community is very important, for without it, chaos rules, and the Spirit is hampered to move as He wills.

All of these ideas are spiritual spinach. Eat your spinach, or you won't grow up big and strong in the Lord!

XVII

Where Does It Stop?

Two of the students with whom I had direct contact, Pat Orsino and Jim Single, had begun to attend our prayer meetings. Pat was a lively junior girl. She became deeply involved in the whole charismatic movement and tried very hard to become an apostle to her classmates and friends. Through her, I learned the importance of being a responsible, loving, and generous servant to those whom the Lord leads to the Pentecostal experience. Just because a person begins attending prayer meetings doesn't mean that his problems have been solved; in fact, he continues to have questions and problems, and he needs someone to help him with them.

In my own experience, I had often asked the question, "Where does it stop?" The Lord had answered in His own way: "It doesn't!"

Jesus wants us to enter into a deeper relationship with Him every day. He wants us to become more and more as He is, holy and perfect. But man can't make himself perfect and holy as God is. God Himself must bring about our perfection, and He will if we let Him: "For God is at work in you, both to will and to work for his good pleasure" (Phil. 2:13). Holiness and perfection are part of a continuous process. "May the God of peace himself sanctify you wholly; and may your spirit and soul and body be kept sound and blameless at the coming of our Lord Jesus Christ. He who calls you is faithful, and he will do it" (I Thess. 5:23-24). Just as Jesus is the One who redeems us and baptizes us in the Holy Spirit, so too, He is the One who perfects us. Our part is to be patient, cooperative, submitting to His perfecting grace.

Graduation day is a big event at Gloucester Catholic High School. The most colorful part of the ceremony is the academic procession in which the faculty members, resplendent in the robes and hoods of their various academic degrees, join with the graduates in a glorious display. I had received my doctor's degree in the previous weeks, making me the holder of the highest degree on the faculty. However, because of a mix-up, my place in the procession was not the position of honor that my degree deserved. My dignity was wounded, but the Lord showed me it is better to trust in the Lord than to trust in earthly powers.

All that God has given us—our natural talents and achievements coupled with prayer and the spiritual gifts—was given in order that the love and glory of God might be revealed to men. As we grow in the use of the gifts of God, we begin to experience God in an ever deeper way. He is always with us. His hand leads and guides us. We become better able to hear His voice when He speaks to us.

Before my summer vacation began in the middle of June, I resolved that at least part of the summer would be spent in writing this book. As I prayed about it, agonizing over the prospect of spending long hours working on the manuscript, I began to understand that the more we come to know and love the Lord and live in His presence, the more we are willing to give our lives over to Him completely.

There may be areas of our lives which are not completely in the Lord. We may be unaware of them, or we may be painfully aware of them without knowing what we ought to do about them. The Lord wants us to be perfect and holy, and so He points out these areas to us so that we can bring them unto the Lord.

For most of us, these areas turn out to be in the areas of obedience to Him and His Church, some secret sin perhaps, and priorities, things which we may still put first before Him. God has to be first in our lives—He won't fit anywhere else—and when we don't put Him first, He shows us through His Spirit. To use a biblical term, He "convicts" us. But God never shows us an area of our life which needs changing without giving us the help we need to change.

Jesus is the one who will ultimately overcome our trials, difficulties, and problems for us. Our role is to admit our weakness and to be patient while the Spirit works within us. Jesus ministers to us both directly and through the pastors of His Church, and leaders and members of our communities. The truth of this came home to me in a very clear way. I was at a prayer meeting at Saint Rose's Church in Haddon Heights, New Jersey, the new and permanent meeting place of the Camden Catholic charismatic community. During the meeting, the trials, difficulties, and problems that had been besetting me for so long seemed to almost overcome me. I fought against asking for prayer, in the falsely prideful conviction that too many present thought that I was so strong that they could always lean on me. But the Lord urged me to humble myself and accept the help which He was ready to give me. I finally broke down and asked for prayer. The result was a tearfully joyous release, a wonderful return to the feelings I experienced when I first received the baptism in the Holy Spirit.

Where does it stop? It doesn't. The Lord continues to teach us forever.

Maranatha! Lord Jesus, come!

XVIII

A Solid Rock

A house built on solid rock withstands all the elements and remains standing. Many outside the charismatic renewal have viewed only its surface appearances and have judged it will pass away. Some of my own colleagues have tolerated my participation in the renewal and told me I would get over it as soon as the novelty wore off. It has been some years now and the renewal holds more meaning than it did when I first became involved. I would like to share with you some theological reflections on the nature of the charismatic renewal. The bulk of what I will say stems from the work of the eminent theologian, Killian McDonnell, from whom I have borrowed freely.*

Those involved in the renewal have as their purpose the proclamation of the gospel and the promised restoration of all men in Christ which "has already begun in Christ, is carried forward in the mission of the Holy Spirit, and through Him continues in the Church" (*Lumen Gentium*, art. 48).

The Catholic charismatic renewal has as its basis the gospel of Jesus Christ. Those in the renewal wish to embrace without reservation the full mystery hidden from all ages in the Father, revealed in the Son, and demonstrated in the Holy Spirit. There is no other gospel than that of Jesus Christ, crucified and risen.

Without wishing to absolutize the events described in the Acts of the Apostles, many see the central theological intuition of the renewal described in Acts. Jesus, crucified and risen, sends the Spirit. "Being therefore exalted at the right hand of God, and having received from the Father the promise of the Holy Spirit, he has poured out this which you see and hear" (Acts 2:32). Jesus both receives and sends the Spirit. The outpouring of the Spirit results in baptism (Acts 2:38), and the birth of Christian communities (Acts 2:41). These communities are built up by the teaching of the apostles, fellowship (*koinonia*), eucharistic celebration, and common prayer (Acts 2:42). Charisms appear among the apostolic community for the upbuilding of the Church (Acts 2:43). The experience of the Spirit's presence and power is directed specifically to witness and mission, and is related to the Lordship of Jesus (Acts 1:8).

Those in the renewal do not seek to isolate certain New Testament doctrines, practices, or charisms in order to give them a greater role than they have in the New Testament witness. The New Testament itself does not isolate the Spirit or His visible activity in the charisms from the other aspects of the Kingdom of God. Both the Spirit and His gifts are integral to the gospel of Jesus and were accepted by the New Testament communities as normal parts of Christian life and ecclesial experience.

The renewal does not purport to bring to the Church something she does not have, but to bring her to release that which she already possesses . . . .

Our hearing of the gospel takes place within a tradition and history which have formed us and of which we are a part. The tradition joins us to the gospel while the history separates us from the gospel—as it was preached and experienced in the early Church.

The Church preaches the same gospel that the early Apostles preached. But the renewal asks if the history out of which we come has not distorted our awareness and expectations so that our response to that gospel has been diminished. For example, if our awareness of what it means to be "in Christ" and "to walk in the Spirit" differs from that of the early Church, and if we have more limited expectations than they did of how the Spirit is visible in the charisms for the service of the Church and the world, then wouldn't this have a profound effect upon the Church's worship, evangelization, and engagement in the life of the world? Those within the charismatic renewal make no claim to a special spiritual endowment, or grace, which distinguishes them from others not so involved. The difference is in their awareness and expectations—and therefore in their experience. The purpose of the renewal is not to bring to the Church something she does not have, but to widen her expectations.

If Catholic charismatics were asked in more specific terms to describe the theological basis of the renewal, they would maintain that theological research and reflection alone are not sufficient means to reach a final answer. The Holy Spirit, because He is "Breath," is less susceptible to analysis than Jesus, who is "Word." However, we will attempt to give some theological explanation that is, in the best tradition of Catholic theology, unashamedly sacramental, but which is offered without prejudice to other explanations.

The Spirit and the charism are regular constituents of the Church, not additions to an already existing body of Christ. In their absence the Church cannot exist. And it holds equally that no group or movement within the Church can claim exclusive hold on the Spirit and His charisms.

St. Paul defines the Christian in terms of both Christ and the

109

Spirit (Rom. 8:9; Col. 1:27). In the gospels what distinguishes the messianic role of Jesus from the role of John the Baptist is that Jesus baptizes in the Holy Spirit. In particular, by the sacrament of baptism one becomes a member of the body of Christ because in baptism one receives the Spirit. "For by one Spirit we were all baptized into one body—Jews or Greeks, slaves or free—and all were made to drink of the one Spirit" (I Cor. 12:13). The New Testament describes in various ways the process by which one becomes a Christian—a process under the aegis of faith. The anointing of faith (I John 2:20, 27) precedes and accompanies conversion, which is a turning "to God from idols, to serve the living and true God, and to wait for his Son from heaven, whom he raised from the dead . . ." (I Thess. 1:9-10). Conversion leads to baptism, the forgiveness of sins, and the receiving of the Holy Spirit (Acts 2:37, 38).

Around these steps of initiation, and subsequent "walking in the Spirit" (Gal. 5:16), we can group many of the other New Testament expressions that refer to the process of becoming a Christian: baptism (Rom. 6), illumination (Heb. 6:4), baptism in the Holy Spirit (Acts 1:5), new creaturehood (Gal. 6:15), filling with the Holy Spirit (Acts 2:4), reception of the Spirit (Gal. 3:2), receiving the gifts and call of God (Rom. 11:29), entrance into the new covenant (Heb. 12:24), new birth (I Pet. 1:23; John 3:3), being born of water and the Spirit (John 3:5).

The coming of the Spirit that decisively constitutes a man as a Christian is related to the celebration of the Christian initiation (baptism, confirmation, Eucharist). The early Christian communities not only received the Spirit during the celebration of initiation, but expected that the Spirit would demonstrate His power by transforming their lives. Further, they expected that the Spirit would come to visibility in the community along the full spectrum of His charisms, which included, but was by no means limited to helping, administration, prophecy, and tongues (I Cor. 12:28; cf. Rom. 12:6-8).

The charisms of the Spirit are without number and constitute the means by which each member of the Church serves the whole body. Charisms are largely directed outward for the building up of the body and its service to the world. Less frequently they are directed inward toward the edification of the individual. Hence we can see the Spirit as He works in each Christian to make of him a servant to the Church and the world.

Unlike the early Church, the contemporary Church is not aware that all the charisms of the Spirit are real possibilities for its life. Its restricted expectations are in part attributable to its tendency to describe the assistance of the Holy Spirit primarily in terms of the hierarchical ministry. But whatever the reasons may be, if the expectation is limited, so will be the experience of the Spirit in the Church's life. And if the Church's experience of the Spirit has become limited, then so has its ability to give witness to Christ unto the uttermost parts of the earth (Acts 1:8). Hence spokesmen for the charismatic renewal maintain that there is an urgent need for the Church to widen its expectations of what the Spirit might do in its midst. They, however, do not wish to restrict the Church's theological and pastoral attention to the charisms per se, because they recognize that the gifts of the Spirit are not ends in themselves. Instead the charisms contribute to that fullness of life in Christ and the Holy Spirit to which the Church is called. The charismatic renewal, therefore, has its theological foundation in the celebration of initiation and calls for a renewal of baptismal consciousness broadly conceived, "That we might understand the gifts bestowed on us by God" (I Cor. 2:12).

Questions Raised by Outsiders

The charismatic renewal is based on the assumption that the Holy Spirit is sovereign and free. He acts when, where, and how He wills. Though the Spirit takes persons and local churches where they are, He is not radically dependent on the subjective dispositions of those persons or communities. The Holy Spirit retains the initiative at every moment of the community's life.

I have already mentioned the more limited expectations of many in the contemporary Church in comparison to the wider expectations of the early Church. The normal experience of renewal inevitably causes the participants to turn their attention to the life of the New Testament churches. However commendable this return to the New Testament witness is, it should not be forgotten that in the course of the Church's history the Holy Spirit and His charisms have never been absent. The Holy Spirit has manifested Himself in a multiplicity of ways in various epochs of the Church. One could mention the lay monastic movements, the founding of religious orders, the prayer gifts in the Church's mystical tradition, the social awareness as manifested in the papal encyclicals, and the movements of political and social engagement. Though the modality in which the Spirit is manifesting Himself today appears to take a new form, it is inaccurate to maintain that the charismatic manifestations began with the Catholic charismatic renewal.

Tongues

While many of the charisms present no problems to persons not involved in the charismatic renewal, the charism of tongues does. The issue of the renewal is not tongues, and the Catholic renewal is not characterized by an insistence that speaking in tongues is in any necessary way tied to the spiritual realities received in initiation. On the other hand persons involved in the renewal rightly point out that this charism was quite common in the New Testament communities. Those who stand

112

outside the renewal and attempt to evaluate the charism of tongues will fail if it is not understood in the framework of prayer. It is essentially a prayer gift enabling many using it to pray at a deeper level. If those within the movement esteem this charism, it is because they want to pray more effectively. For a sizeable number of persons who pray in tongues, this is only one of a number of forms of prayer. They also engage in liturgical prayer, eucharistic celebrations, and other forms of public and private devotion. This charism, whose existence in the New Testament communities and in early post-apostolic times is well attested, should be neither exalted nor despised.

Holy Spirit Baptism

Another feature of the renewal which causes confusion is the use of the phrase "baptism in the Holy Spirit." For historical reasons, many Catholics in the renewal have adopted this phrase, already current among classical Pentecostals, to describe the experience through which they came into a new awareness of the presence and power of the Spirit in their lives.

But there is a problem in the use of the phrase. It could be taken to mean that only those who have had a particular kind of experience of the Spirit have really been baptized in the Spirit. This is not the case, since every valid and fruitful Christian initiation confers "the gift of the Holy Spirit" (Acts 2:38), and "to be baptized in the Holy Spirit" is simply another scriptural way of saying "to receive the Holy Spirit."

Hence, many prefer to use other expressions to describe what is happening in the charismatic renewal. Among the alternatives which have been proposed are: "the release of the Spirit," "renewal of the sacraments of initiation," "a release of the power to witness to the faith," "actualization of gifts already received in potency," "manifestation of baptism whereby the hidden grace given in baptism breaks through into conscious experience," "reviviscence of the sacraments of initiation." These are all ways of saying that the power of the Holy Spirit, given in Christian initiation, but hitherto unexperienced, becomes a matter of personal, conscious experience.

Whatever one may call this experience, it can happen without any emotional elevation. The experience, although it may evoke feelings, should not be equated with them. Further, this release or emergence of the graces of initiation into conscious experience can be a gradual process, without any strong emotional overtones.

Besides this growth pattern of experience, there is what might be called a crisis pattern. This occurs when one can precisely date the moment when the graces of initiation emerged into conscious experience. The crisis pattern is less familiar to Catholic theological cultures, but it is in fact common to many Catholics within the renewal. Both the growth pattern and the crisis pattern should be looked upon as authentic ways of realizing the graces of initiation at the conscious level.

Personal Commitment

There are many objective elements in the renewal as in the whole Catholic tradition: the celebration of initiation, obedience to the teaching and discipline of the magisterium of the Church, eucharistic celebration, the sacrament of penance, and the sacred Scriptures. But one of the most notable aspects of the renewal is its insistence on a largely subjective matter: personal commitment. As an adult, one cannot be a Christian by proxy. Each adult must say his own personal yes to the baptism received as an infant. This emphasis is in keeping with the more personal and explicit adherence to faith taught by *Gaudium et Spes*, art. 7. The constitution speaks of "a more critical ability to distinguish religion from a magical view of the world and from the superstitions which still circulate." This more critical ability "purifies religion and exacts day by day a more personal and explicit adherence to faith. As a result, many persons are achieving a more vivid sense of God."

One of the great strengths of the renewal is its insistence on a genuine conversion experience which leads to living faith, profound love of prayer, love of the Eucharist, new appreciation for the sacrament of penance, healing of interpersonal relationships, moral transformation, renewed sense of discipleship, awareness of the necessity of firm doctrinal basis, and fidelity to the bishops and to the Pope. In some places, especially in Latin America, involvement in the charismatic renewal has meant a new level of engagement in social and political programs. Pervading all these areas is the sense of the presence of the person of Christ, the power of the Spirit, and the glory of the Father. The response to His presence is, most characteristically, praise.

Conclusion

The strengths of the renewal may be instruments for the transformation of the interior life of the Church. Many people need a new assurance of faith and a renewed life of prayer. It is well known that many have ceased to pray. This is true even of priests.

The strengths of the renewal can lead to social and political action based not on class hatred, but love and prayer for the oppressors. This in no way lessens the struggle against the evils of poverty and violence. It means instead a more radically Christian style of social and political action wherein God's omnipotence is released to accomplish what men have failed to do.

A weakness of the renewal lies in uncritical acceptance of prophecy and tongues without sufficient discernment as to what comes from the Holy Spirit and what comes from the psyche. It should be remembered that the final judgment as to the authenticity of charisms "belongs to those who preside over the Church and to whose special competence it belongs not indeed to extinguish the Spirit, but to test all things and hold fast to that which is good" (*Lumen Gentium*, art. 12).

There is also present in some quarters an exaggerated supernaturalism with regard to the charisms, together with an undue preoccupation with them. This is evidenced by those who attribute too quickly to demonic influence a manifestation which is judged not to be of God. Then, in another sphere, there are those who imply that when one has the gospel one does not need the Church. Over against them, and equally reprehensible, are those who oppose the subjective experience of salvation to the celebration of the sacraments. Another cause for concern is that insufficient attention is sometimes paid to the theological training of persons whom the various communities judge to be called to specific ministries. In fact, some place in false opposition the transforming power of the Spirit and theological training. One also laments the reluctance among some leaders to listen carefully to criticism—admittedly a nearly universal foible. Finally, some within the renewal have not drawn the inevitable social implications of life in Christ and the Spirit. In some cases there is social engagement, but it is largely superficial and does not come to grips with the problems of oppression and injustice.

An attempt has been made to formulate the most widely accepted view of the theological-sacramental basis of the renewal—a view based in the celebration of initiation. I have made some miscellaneous observations about the strengths of the renewal and about its specific problems. A final word should be said about the relation of the Catholic charismatic renewal to other renewals. Those involved in the Catholic renewal recognize that there are other renewals within other

Christian communities and churches, as well as outside of them, which give quite different theological explanations for the same experiences. Even though the theological formulations vary, and even though the understanding of Christian revelation differs in important ways, those within the Catholic renewal recognize the presence of the Spirit in those who proclaim the lordship of Jesus to the glory of the Father. That presence in all streams of the renewal is the bond of their unity.

---

*This chapter is drawn in substance from McDonnell's *Statement of the Theological Basis of the Catholic Charismatic Renewal* available in leaflet form from Inter Faith House, Box 13, Louisville, Ky. 40201.

XIX

A Personal Vision

Many have asked me what I think about David Wilkerson's much publicized *Vision*. Frankly, its content and the manner in which it has been publicized force me to suspend judgment as to its validity. I do, however, have my own personal vision of the future of the charismatic renewal, especially in the Catholic church.

I see in the charismatic renewal today an increasing emphasis on the lordship of Jesus—with the result that many Christians are beginning to reorder priorities in their lives. And this reordering of our own lives is significantly restructuring our Christian witness.

Once a person has accepted Jesus as his personal Savior and consciously decided to submit all areas of his life to the lordship of Jesus, he is then led to participate in a Christian community wherein he experiences a sharing of the new life and the operation of the Holy Spirit's gifts. After a thorough grounding in the basic truths with the support of the community, the Christian is then led to serve his own community, and the wider community of the Church through a specific ministry discerned by himself or the community, *and* confirmed by the community.

A Pentecostal Christian, then, is one who is living under the lordship of Jesus through and in the power of Pentecost in a community of believers.

Lordship of Jesus

Immediately following the first Pentecost, Peter preached a sermon in the power of the Spirit. As a result of that Spirit-powered preaching, his listeners were convinced of their own need, so they cried out: "What must we do?" Peter answered: "Repent, and be baptized every one of you in the name of Jesus Christ for the forgiveness of your sins: and you shall receive the gift of the Holy Spirit."

This simple message is the key we need today to enter and abide in the kingdom of God. But how do I make this key work? What does it mean to come under the lordship of Jesus? To repent? To receive the Holy Spirit?

Practically speaking, repentance does not mean so much remorse for past life or sins as a willingness to submit my life to the rule of Jesus. It is a decision to give everything I am, everything I have, to Jesus. I do this once at some point in my life, and I continue to do it as often as I realize the need. Repentance means to seek God first, and relying on Him to take care of the practical details of life.

But how do I know if repentance is needed? Simply by asking myself these questions:

1. Who is first in my life?
   a. Is it myself?
   b. Is it my wife or husband?
   c. Is it my children?
   d. Is it my parents?
   e. Is it someone else I feel I love and can't give up?
   or is it Jesus???

2. How do I find out who is first in my life? Simple. What or who fills my imagination most? With what or whom do I spend most of my time? Not the time I must spend at my job or duties, but my *free time*? Where and on what do I spend my own personal money?

If I find that Jesus is not first in my life, in *all* areas of my life including my relationships with others, my thoughts, my imagination, my sexuality, what must I do? Every day I must make a conscious act of submission to Jesus. I must have enough boldness of faith to say: "Here I am, Lord! Take me! I give You all that I am."

In the daily living of repentance I must trust that the Holy Spirit will convict me of sin in those areas of my life that I have not yielded completely or that need daily yielding to the Lord. How will this take place? Wherever I lose my peace—that is where I find sin. In Galatians 5, Paul describes the criteria for the normal Christian life, the fruits of the Spirit: love, peace, faithfulness, kindness, joy, patience, meekness, gentleness and self-control. Whenever these are missing, there is sin, and the Holy Spirit is calling me to submit that area of unrest to the lordship of Jesus.

As Pentecostals, we claim that we have received the baptism in the Holy Spirit. This means that we have consciously and deliberately sought for the release of the Holy Spirit and His power in our lives. As a result, the Holy Spirit has manifested His possession of us through the operation of the spiritual gifts (tongues, healing, prophecy, etc.). But yielding to the will of the Holy Spirit is not a one-shot deal. Certainly we receive the baptism in the Spirit once we ask for it, and experience its effects in proportion to how much we have yielded at the time; but yielding to the Spirit is a continuing experience, a daily release of His power, a continual baptism in the Spirit.

Yielding to the Holy Spirit leads us into the eternal childhood of believers. "Unless you become like little children, you shall not enter the kingdom." This requirement deeply challenges the American ideal of independence: "I'd rather do it myself!" It means becoming as dependent as an infant in the things of the Lord. It is the heartfelt prayer of one who knows he is helpless, "You lead me, Lord!" It means waiting on the Holy Spirit so that my speaking in tongues, prophecy or interpretation are authentic. On the other side of the same coin is a faith-principle that must be in operation lest we fall into the error of quietism. It says, "You get as much as you expect." While we passively wait on the Lord in a certain circumstance, that passivity must be set in an active faith that says, "I believe the Lord will lead me, and when He does, I will obey." We must become participants in a continuing process of basic initiation as an ongoing feature of our Christian communities. There is no better method than the one found in the Scriptures:

Kerygma*

Proclaim the gospel—Jesus is Lord! Our Christian communities must become centers for the study and practice of the Word of God. A very useful tool to begin the process is a "Life in the Spirit Seminar" taught by a revolving team of teachers who teach what they have learned. The lessons must be practical, concrete, and find living expression in the lives of those teaching. An old Latin adage sums it up: *nemo dat quod non habet,* "no one can give what he doesn't have." This means that those who fulfill the teaching role in the proclamation of the Word had better be living what they proclaim. We must acknowledge that the majority of nominal Christians have not been evangelized, and many others have not so much as heard the full gospel message. So our primary task is to evangelize families, friends, and fellow church members. These are people who have known us too well. For most of them the most effective evangelization will consist of the gospel they see changing us, our actions and our attitudes. If and when they *see* the truth of the Good News lived in us, then perhaps they will be more easily convinced of its reality.

Didache*

In *didache* the information passed on through the *kerygma* is appropriated. The lordship and redemption of Jesus is personally made an integral part and center of the Christian's life. This appropriation takes place when the neophyte, the newly reborn and Spirit-baptized Christian, enters into serious relationship with a group of those who have been living the new life for some time. It is in and through the small growth group that the neophyte begins to see the implications of Christ's reign in his life by observing the lives of his brothers and sisters and listening to their advice. An excellent tool to present the basic principles to be learned and appropriated during this growth period are the "Foundations Courses I and II" prepared by the New Life Community in Ann Arbor, Michigan.

Discipleship

Ordinarily, we judge that a person is a believer if he does three things:
  a. Attends church services regularly;
  b. Supports his church financially;
  c. Tries to live a holy life.
But these criteria would be the same for the member of any club. Isn't the Church more than a club? Isn't it the body of Christ? A believer is a member of a body, not simply a club. Biology tells us that a member of the body takes in life and

passes it on through circulation and cell production under the direction of the nervous system, controlled by the brain. It is the same in the body of Christ. We as members take in life, His life, and reproduce ourselves by passing on that life under direction from the Head. Christ's last command was, "Go, therefore and make disciples of all nations . . . !" A disciple is one who is taught (*kerygma*) and formed (*didache*) so that he may teach and form others under Christ's direction. When St. Paul wrote, "Imitate me," he was not being proud. He knew it was the pattern God had ordained. Real discipling cannot be accomplished with throngs of people. The Lord Himself evangelized thousands but discipled only twelve. Those twelve, in turn, discipled a further seventy-two.

This means that priests and lay leaders in the Catholic charismatic renewal must curtail their leadership roles with large groups and concentrate on smaller ones. This is taking one step backward so as to be able to take two steps forward. Leaders in the charismatic renewal will increasingly find their energies dissipated unless they are willing to commit themselves to a few rather than to many. This will consititute a sore blow to the sense of self-importance that plagues most leaders. They must refuse to become involved in outside interests no matter how "charismatic." They must further realize that they are not the star of the show. Jesus is the only star and He will accomplish His ministry through His body. Discipleship is the most time-consuming and trying way to build that body, but it is Christ's way.

A priest or layman who has emerged as a leader in a prayer group should pick a few disciples only after much prayer and reflection. He should enter into serious covenant with them and, under the headship of Christ, share with them, intimately and candidly, what God has taught him by real experience—not by books. In time, these budding disciples will have experienced some things themselves and be ready to

124

"teach others also." As discipleship grows, so will the body, solidly and soundly.

Such discipling cells must be squarely under the authority of the local church; that is probably one good reason to nurture leadership in the priests, so that the whole work may tie the movement in with the institutional church. In this way we can begin to see the total vision of the whole Church charismatically renewed both in structure and operation.

The implications of this basic message for the whole Church are unlimited. Local churches could be entirely restructured according to the pattern of evangelization, formation, and discipleship. Pastors and priests could be transformed by the Spirit and take up the task of living and preaching the Gospel no longer caught up in bureaucratic detail and the vain effort to raise funds from uncommitted, unevangelized, and nominal Christians. Evangelized, Spirit-filled Christians don't have to be persuaded or coerced by professional fund-raisers to support the life and works of the Church. Such giving is merely the logical expression of genuine discipleship. The ordinary parishioner can become totally involved in the proclamation of the gospel through his own experience of it, and the ongoing experience of the gifts and fruits of the Spirit. Imagine the office of apostle-bishop, the presbyterate, and the parish renewed by the Spirit in terms of evangelization, formation, and discipleship. Imagine Catholic education being restructured according to the scriptural model of *kerygma*, *didache*, and discipleship. The final purpose of the charismatic renewal is not to form permanent prayer groups, but alternate supportive non-permanent communities which will facilitate the restructuring of Christian institution to enliven and broaden the body of Christ. This is the long-range goal of the charismatic renewal. We must be committed to work toward it. Meanwhile, our immediate commitment is undoubtedly to evangelization—telling and living the Good News. By obeying the Spirit one step at a time we will see the total vision come about in God's way at God's time.

---

* *Kerygma* is a Greek word that means *proclamation* or *announcement* (commonly pronounced kah-*rig*-mah).

* *Didache* is a Greek word that means *teaching* or *instruction* (commonly pronounced *di*-dah-kay).

XX

The Catholic Pentecostal Community

I believe that the establishment of Catholic Pentecostal prayer communities is a manifestation of a divine impulse within the Roman Catholic church wherein spontaneous communities or diaspora churches are coming to birth. Thus two ecclesiologies are emerging—the official, classic model in force from the Middle Ages to Vatican II, and the new, still experimental model of marginal community—which at times will be in conflict with each other. However, I believe that one and the same faith is lived, experienced, and given historical form in official church structures and in the unofficial Pentecostal groupings.

What has happened with the establishment of Catholic Pentecostal communities is bound to happen more frequently in the future and is throwing more light on a new way of understanding and accepting the full scope of the Christian gospel. My thesis is that besides the classic model of church, another model, equally historical in its own way, is emerging in our day. The role of priest and bishop, the concept of the unity of the church, liturgy, and the exercise of ministry are interpreted and lived differently. If any one model is seized on as absolute, conflict is inevitable.

The principal elements of a Catholic Pentecostal community are about the same as the first Christian communities—the celebration of the Eucharist, reading of the Word of God, prayer in common, and the exercise of the charismatic gifts and ministries.

One of the primary concerns for the Catholic Pentecostal community should be for the complete liberation of men in Christ, and it is from this vantage point that it must confront the concept of hierarchy. One of the major obstacles to freedom in Christ is the religious oppression practiced by some churchmen. The task of the Catholic Pentecostal community is to search for the means of integrating itself with faith in Christ today, and to reject the idea that any one individual or group—bishops or theologians—can think and decide for everyone, everywhere.

The Catholic Pentecostal community does not have an attitude of resentment, rancor, or the will to destroy the institution as such. What it represents is resistance to a religious structure which stifles freedom, and adherence to the search in common of faith understood as a deep participation in the Spirit of Christ, in the struggle of men for the realization of justice and fraternity, the furthering of the kingdom of God. The Catholic Pentecostal community does not want to place itself outside the pale of the Church of Christ as it is now established, but it must be a witness to freedom in confrontation with all the forms of authoritarianism and legalism dominating the Church.

The Pentecostal community lives in the hope that the Holy Spirit will again give life to the dry bones of ecclesiastical structure and should, as a logical consequence, with boldness and love, break with every type of abuse of power and oppression. They should break with anything clerical that sees the unity of believers as a servile observance to human legislation imposed in the name of God. They should distinguish between communion within the church and supine acquiescence in the dogmatic disciplinary power of the sacerdotal caste.

Union with Christ and with the church does not mean, always and everywhere, union with a hierarchy intent only on wielding without contest a power alleged to be an expression of the will of God.

I believe that the Pentecostal movement is a genuine move of the Holy Spirit inviting individuals to a deeper and lasting personal relationship to Jesus Christ. Even if this means eventually a reinterpretation of the nature of the Church and its varied ministries, we must be open to what the Holy Spirit is doing and not constrain His action by our theological prejudices. We must move in faith and pray, "Lord Jesus, come!" and be willing to take the risks that this entails. Even if this incurs the temporary displeasure or condemnation of ecclesiastical superiors, we must "obey God, rather than men."

I believe the Holy Spirit is the Spirit of love and of unity, therefore I don't believe that the Pentecostal experience should be a wedge between an individual and his own church. There is no doubt that it will cause tension, but tension is a sign of life. A dead body doesn't have any tension at all. The Catholic Pentecostal should integrate himself within a living expression of the new life and power he has received, so that this new life can be nurtured and guided through the delicate system of checks and balances found in a Catholic Pentecostal community. The Catholic Pentecostal community, in turn, should integrate itself within the existing structure of the larger community, the institutional Church, so that its new life and power may receive the guidance and direction it needs to be the effective vehicle through which the whole Church may be revitalized. In 1969 at a special commission from all the Catholic bishops in the United States, this Pentecostal movement within the Catholic Church was given official approval. There are over 50,000 Catholic Pentecostals in the Church today.

There is nothing more discouraging to me than a Christian having this wonderful transforming experience and then running away from his own church. It is like winning a fabulous amount of money and then refusing to share it with the members of your own family—it's really unfair. I believe that if we are really to cooperate with what Jesus in His Holy Spirit is doing today, we will dismiss any thought of starting any super-denominational church or a new reformation. Rather, we will boldly and consistently live our new experience and become the fire by which the whole Church of God will once again become kindled from within. Whether you are Catholic or Protestant, there are community Pentecostal Fellowships in your area.

If you are a Catholic, I suggest that you go to a Catholic Pentecostal meeting, where you will feel at home and relaxed. An excellent international directory of these groups is published and revised annually by Charismatic Renewal Services.

Write to them at P.O. Box 617, Ann Arbor, Michigan 48107, for further information.

Why not try it for yourself? You have nothing to lose except defeat and everything to gain in the abundant life that Jesus will give in response to your faith.

XXI

Understanding the New Life:
A Glossary

As the charismatic renewal (or modern Pentecostal movement) has developed, certain words and phrases have cropped up that convey definite meanings. This final chapter will list the most commonly used terms with their important meanings.

1. Salvation Experience, The New Birth: "You Must Be Born Again," accepting Jesus as Lord and Savior:

There is nothing more disconcerting or disturbing than to have someone suddenly come up to you and abruptly ask, "Have you been saved?" If you belong to any of the major denominations, especially the sacramentarian churches, your answer might be something like, "Saved from what?" What your zealous questioner is trying to find out is: Have you had a real personal encounter with Jesus?

For those of us in the historic sacramentarian churches, such as the Catholic, Episcopal, Lutheran, Presbyterian, Orthodox, etc., there is no question of compromise in our belief that when we were baptized we were engrafted into the Mystical Body of Christ. Most of us were baptized as infants and have accepted the teaching of our church that this baptism washed away our original sin and placed us in a new relationship with Jesus Christ our Savior.

What the question means for us is: Have we ever made a mature and determined decision to make actual in our conscious life what Jesus did for us in sacramental baptism?

We read in the New Testament that there is a distinct experience of salvation available to anyone who seeks it. The Catholic church has taught about this experience in its teaching on the *Baptism of Desire.*

Those involved in the charismatic renewal say that this experience is indispensable to a fully conscious and deliberate Christian life. It is the first step to union with God, to the "abundant life" that Jesus promises.

How does one go about receiving this wonderful, liberating experience?

a. Accept God's word: that He loves you and wants to give you an abundant life (John 3:16; 10:10).

b. Accept God's word: that you are a sinner and that this separates you from God (Rom. 3:23; 6:23).

c. Admit that you've been wrong and ask the Father to take away your guilt by the blood of Jesus.

d. Ask Jesus to come into your life and become your Savior and Lord.

e. Believe He has come the minute you ask Him. Thank Him for saving you and giving you new life.

Here is the chance to experience for yourself what pleases the Lord and brings you into a vital relationship with Him. If you decide, here is a simple prayer you might use:

"Father, I believe that Jesus Christ is your only begotten Son, and that He became a human being, shed His blood and died on the Cross to cleanse away my guilt and sin that was separating me from you. I believe that He rose from the dead, physically, to give me new life. Lord Jesus, I invite you to come

132

into my heart. I accept you as my Savior and Lord. I confess my sinfulness and ask you to wash me with you blood. I believe that you have come and are living in me right now. Thank you, Jesus!"

When you pray this prayer from your heart, you may actually feel something happen, or you may not, but what you feel matters no more than the waves on the surface of the ocean; your "spirit" which comes alive through Jesus dwells in a place far deeper than emotions. Whether you feel anything immediately or not, you will soon find that you *are* different because Jesus will do what He promised. He keeps His word.

2. The Baptism in the Holy Spirit; Personal Pentecost:

All Christians who have had the aforementioned salvation experience have access to a subsequent spiritual experience that can complete and strengthen them. As the church developed, this second experience, referred to in Scripture as the baptism in the Holy Spirit, became the sacrament of confirmation. On the Feast of the Assumption, August 15, 1971, Pope Paul VI issued a revised rite of confirmation. This new decree included a significant statement: ". . . ordinarily the sacrament is administered by the bishop so that there will be a more evident relationship to the first outpouring of the Holy Spirit on the day of Pentecost. After they were filled with the Holy Spirit, the apostles themselves gave the Spirit to the faithful through the laying on of their hands. In this way, the reception of the Spirit through the ministry of the bishop shows the close bond which joins the confirmed to the Church and the mandate of Christ to be witnesses among men."

The Catholic church believes that Jesus acts in a direct way through the sacraments. In this statement we can see the special relationship between the baptism in the Holy Spirit and confirmation; the one is an experience deeply personal and individual, the other is a communal experience tying its

133

recipient to the body of believers. But in both it is Jesus Christ who acts, who baptizes in the Holy Spirit.

We believe that we receive the Holy Spirit in (baptism or) regeneration, but in the baptism in the Holy Spirit or confirmation, He is poured out to overflowing. The gift of the Holy Spirit is for everyone who accepts Christ. He embodies the power necessary for the fullness of the Christian life, the power to transform us that we will more and more have the mind of Christ.

As we yield ourselves to the Spirit of God, our hearts will be so set aflame with love for our fellowman and with love for Jesus that we will more and more "show forth" His praise, not only with our lips, but in our lives, by giving up ourselves to "His" service, and by walking before "Him" in holiness and righteousness all our days.

When we receive the baptism in the Holy Spirit we receive the promise of the Father and are endued with power from on high; we are equipped to enter into the Spirit-led life. We shall then witness the nine gifts of the Spirit, manifested for the building up of the body of Christ: the word of wisdom, the word of knowledge, faith, gifts of healing, the working of miracles, prophecy, the discerning of spirits, divers kinds of tongues, and interpretation of tongues.

The Pentecostal experience, then, is an experience of consciously allowing the Holy Spirit to overflow in and through us by the action of faith in the promise of Jesus Christ. Like the experience of salvation or being born again, it is a faith experience accompanied by the manifestation of a new level of spiritual life. This experience can be appropriated by faith as the inherited right of the Christian believer.

Before asking Jesus for this experience, there is an important step that must be taken. The first and most important commandment that God gave us is, "I am the Lord thy God and thou shalt not have any strange gods before me. . . ."

Many of us, consciously or unconsciously, have broken this commandment by delving into the counterfeit spiritual world of the occult, e.g., astrology, hypnotism, ouija board, mind expansion courses, astral projection, witchcraft, secret societies, drugs, etc. Through these acts we have opened our spirits to occult bondage by which Satan blocks the acquisition of a full and free life in the Holy Spirit.

I believe that a simple prayer of deliverance will free us of all obstacles to the full reception of the Holy Spirit and the manifestation of His gifts:

"Father in Heaven, I confess and repent of involvement in (name those you know of), and if I have believed, studied, or practiced anything else that is displeasing to you or contrary to your word, I am truly sorry. I ask you to forgive me for being involved in these things and I promise you that I will not have anything more to do with them. And if I have any books or equipment connected with them, I promise you I will burn them right away.

"I renounce these false cults and teachings in the name of Jesus Christ. Any spirit of false religion, I bind by the power and authority in the name of Jesus and cast you into outer darkness, never to return."

Now you are ready to ask Jesus to baptize you in the Holy Spirit.

a. Ask Jesus to baptize you in the Holy Spirit. You must ask.

b. Believe that you will receive this baptism the moment you ask: "Ask and you shall receive that your joy may be full" (John 16:24). Remember that receiving is something *you* do.

c. Confess with your lips. When you received Jesus as Savior, you believed in your heart and confessed Him with your lips. Now confess the Holy Spirit with your lips, but in the new language that the Lord is ready to give you. Open your mouth and show that you believe the Lord has baptized you in the Spirit by beginning to speak as the Holy Spirit gives you the utterance, and thank God for fulfilling His promise to you. Don't speak in any language you know; God can't guide you to speak in tongues if you are speaking in a language known to you. Trust God to give you the sounds. It is simply speaking, using your voice, but instead of saying what your mind wants you to say, you trust the Holy Spirit to take your voice—surrender. "Open your mouth and I will fill it!" (Ps. 81:10).

If you would rather follow a prayer than make up your own, this one will do:

"Heavenly Father, I thank you that I am under the protection of the precious blood of Jesus which has cleansed me from all sin. Dear Lord Jesus, baptize me in the Holy Spirit and let me praise God in a new language beyond the limitations of my mind. Thank you, Lord; I believe that you are doing this right now. In Jesus' name I ask."

3. The Gifts or Manifestations of the Holy Spirit (I Cor. 12-14):

a. Teaching Gifts: The word of wisdom and the word of knowledge—these are special inspirations by which God works through one person to give understanding to another person or to a group of people. It is then either a lesson or instruction to a Christian assembly of believers or a special word of advice or instruction to a particular person.

The utterance of wisdom and knowledge are spiritual gifts that work through the understanding. The Spirit inspires a person to understand a truth, to understand things the way God understands them, and then to speak about them. There is a difference between natural understanding, acquired by study, and inspired understanding. Inspired understanding feeds the spirit in a way that natural understanding cannot, because it is a manifestation of the presence of the Spirit in a person. I makes a deep change in people, giving them an increase of spiritual life.

b. Sign Gifts: The next three gifts which Saint Paul mentions could be called sign gifts: faith, gifts of healing, and the working of miracles. They are gifts which manifest the power of God in the world in a particular striking way. They call attention to God's reality, and so they bring people to a knowledge of God. The words of Christ at the end of the Gospel of Mark tell us that this is God's way of confirming the truth of the message (as Aquinas pointed out, such confirmation is important if men are to be able to accept the truth of something that is beyond human reason):

"Go into all the world and preach the gospel to the whole creation. He who believes and is baptized will be saved; but he who does not believe will be condemned. And these signs will accompany those who believe: in my name they will cast out demons. They will speak in new tongues; they will pick up serpents; and if they drink any deadly thing, it will not hurt them; they will lay their hands on the sick, and they will recover. . . . And they went forth and preached everywhere, while the Lord worked with them and confirmed the message by the signs that attended it."

The sign gifts are the working of the Spirit in power through certain believers, so that men might know the truth of the Christian gospel. The first of these, the gift of faith, is not the same as the faith by which all Christians believe and turn to Christ. That is given to all Christians, not just to "another." That kind of faith is what makes men Christians. This kind of faith is a special spiritual gift.

1. The charismatic gift of faith seems to be a special gift of prayer. It is a gift of praying with a God-given confidence, and it produces extraordinary results. The person who prays with faith *knows*, through the work of the Spirit in him, that what he asks for will be given. It is the kind of faith which Christ was speaking about when he said in the Gospel of Mark (Mark

11:23), "Truly I say to you, whoever says to this mountain, Be taken up and cast into the sea, and does not doubt in his heart, but believes that what he says will come to pass, it will be done for him."

The gift of faith is what the prophet Elijah had when he confronted the prophets of Baal. He challenged them to a contest. Whoever's God would send down fire from heaven to consume a burnt offering would be the God of Israel. The prophets of Baal went through every rite they could think of, to get Baal to burn the offering, with no results at all. Elijah, on the other hand, first drenched the offering with water so that there would be no doubt about the power of Yahweh, and then he simply prayed, knowing God would answer. And He did. Such faith is God-given. No matter how a man would try to work himself into such faith, he could not do it.

2. The gifts of healing are different from the power of prayer for healing which is part of the ordinary life of the Christian community. Christians pray for one another for a variety of things and see results. In our community, we have seen people cured of migraine headaches from which they have suffered for years, of colds and flu, of epileptic seizures. Not every prayer has been answered, but we have seen far more than can be explained in nonspiritual terms. Moreover, the sacrament of the Anointing of the Sick has always been a normal part of the life of the church, and since the recent outpouring of the Spirit, I know of individuals who were given up as hopeless, who started improving right after receiving the sacrament and are well today. Most priests can give testimonies of the differences the sacrament has made. These things are part of the normal life of the Christian community.

3. There are, however, people who seem to be channels for healing. When they pray for healing, there are results, and they happen with greater frequency and with more extraordinary effect than occur with other believers. The Spirit

works through them to produce "works of power," to produce "things for people to be astonished at," to produce miracles. These people are channels for special spiritual gifts, because God wishes to use them to bring others to know Christ.

c. Revelational Gifts: The next four gifts are gifts which could be called revelational gifts: prophecy, the ability to distinguish between spirits (sometimes called discernment of spirits), various kinds of tongues, and interpretation of tongues. These are gifts by which God makes known something about the present situation to his people.

1. Discernment of spirits has been called the protection of the Christian community. This is the gift which allows a man to "distinguish between spirits," to tell whether an evil spirit is at work in a person or a situation or whether it is the Holy Spirit or whether it is just a man's own spirit. This is probably the work of the Spirit by which Peter "saw" that Simon was "in the gall of bitterness and the bond of iniquity" when he tried to buy the power to confer the Spirit (Acts 8:23), or by which Paul could "see" that the Holy Spirit had given the cripple the faith to be made well (Acts 14:9).

2. Prophecy is a gift by which God speaks through a person a message to an individual or to the whole Christian community. It is God making use of someone to tell men what He thinks about the present situation or what His intention is for the future, or what He thinks they should know or be mindful of right now. Prophecy is not necessarily for foretelling the future (although this frequently happens). Paul describes some of the uses of prophecy by saying in I Cor. 14:3, "He who prophesies, speaks to men for their upbuilding and encouragement and consolation." It is God speaking now to His children, words which are intended to reveal His present purposes.

The term prophecy can be used in many ways, but when Paul used the term prophecy, he did so in such a way that would preclude a person calling it teaching or judging the present situation. He referred specifically to the type of speaking that occurred when one of the prophets at Antioch stated that Paul and Barnabas were to be set aside for apostolic work (Acts 13:2), or when Agabus foretold that there would be a great famine (Acts 11:28), or when Agabus predicted how Paul would be taken prisoner (Acts 21:11).

These prophecies were given as messages from God. They are given in the words of God (the speaker speaks in the first person). That they are more than just human speech is indicated by the accuracy of the predictions and by the fact that the prophet gives directions from God, something that would be sheer presumption if God himself were not speaking. It is clear that not all prophecies are like this. The Book of Acts only reports some of the more extraordinary prophecies, but these are enough to indicate that when the New Testament speaks of prophecy, it uses the word in a special sense to indicate direct messages from God.

Speaking a prophecy is more than a person just saying something that happens to be on his mind as if it were a message from God. The prophet receives a special "anointing"—an urging to speak. He realizes that he has a message from God, although often he does not know what it is until he actually yields to God and begins to speak. To the degree he yields to God, to that degree his message will be pure. And the speaker must be willing to submit the purity of his message to the judgment of those he addresses (I Cor. 14:29). A prophetic message is different from a teaching. A man gives a teaching with his understanding. He sees the truth of what he is saying. A prophet may not understand what he is saying, and he can never "see" that this is God's message right now. He has received a revelation, a message from God.

Prophecy can be very effective in building up the Christian community. It is clear from I Cor. 14 that prophecy was very common in the early church. The church at Corinth apparently had so many messages that there had to be a certain order in giving them (I Cor. 14:29-32). When a prophecy is given at a gathering of Christians, it has a powerful effect in drawing them to God and deepening their sense of the presence of God.

3. Speaking in tongues can be two different things. First of all, it can be a gift of prayer for an individual (I Cor. 14:14). This is the more common gift of tongues, but I will not go into it here. Speaking in tongues can also be a gift for the community when the Spirit urges someone to speak aloud in tongues for the community. In this case, the speaking in tongues must have an interpretation, so that the whole community can understand what is happening.

The experience of giving interpretations is similar to the experience of prophecy. The interpreter, like the speaker in tongues, does not understand the tongues (I Cor. 14:2, 14). In other words, the gift of interpretation is not a gift of translation; it is an urging to speak words which are given.

The charismatic gifts, then, are intended to equip a Christian with supernatural tools for full service in the community, to equip him with the power of God so that he can work in the community with God-given ability to strengthen the community. That is why Paul ends the chapter with the paragraph on apostles, prophets, teachers, workers of miracles, healers, helpers, administrators, speakers in various kinds of tongues. These are the various services Christians can perform in the community, and they are stable positions within a community, needed by the community.

It should also be kept in mind that, while these spiritual gifts are of enormous use wherever Christians minister, for they contain that supernatural power which changes a nonbeliever's heart, when the Christian community is functioning according to scriptural pattern, the community as a body becomes a powerful witness, attracting nonbelievers by the love and manifestation of Jesus in men.

So one way of summarizing the spiritual gifts is to liken them to tools or resources. They are the equipment of God for the work He has given Christians to do in the world. Christians need the power of God to do the work of God, because the work of God is something beyond human ability. The spiritual gifts are the empowering of Christians to do God's work—to teach, to speak His message, to perform signs of His presence, and in all things to glorify the Son. They are the Holy Spirit working through men to renew the face of the earth.

4. Slaying in the Spirit: The first time I came into contact with this phenomenon was at a regional convention of the Full Gospel Business Men's Fellowship International in New York City. Kathryn Kuhlman was to minister at a Miracle Service. I knew nothing of her ministry but was open to the fact that nothing is impossible with God. I took a seat at the rear of the gigantic ballroom of the hotel and was amazed to see more than a thousand expectant people crammed literally from wall to wall.

One of the directors, who was also my friend, saw me and insisted that I take a seat on the platform. Suddenly, the service began. Miss Kuhlman appeared and I was immediately turned off by what I considered her theatricality. Then she began to preach a sermon electrifying both in its content and presentation. All at once a hush fell upon that place as the presence of God became so real that I expected to actually see the resurrected Jesus appear in that room. I asked the Lord to forgive me for having judged Kathryn Kuhlman. Then Kathryn was granted the Spirit's gift of the Word of Knowledge and began to announce the various diseases which people in the assembly were being healed of. She asked those who had experienced healing to come up on the platform to testify. A large line soon formed as men, women, and children came to the microphone to tell of their healing from paralysis, tumors, cancer, and almost every disease imaginable.

After they had spoken, Kathryn would simply touch them and they would fall backwards under the power of the Holy Spirit. They lay there enjoying the glory of the real presence of God until someone assisted them to their feet. As this was going on I simply could not understand what was happening to those people. I said to myself, "If she touches me I won't fall over like that. I don't want to make a spectacle of myself in front of all these people; but I don't have to worry, I have no reason to go near her. I'll just sit here and pray."

That very next moment a woman came to Kathryn to testify that she had been healed of a spinal ailment. She was a middle-aged woman who said she was a Catholic. Kathryn looked over to where I was seated and asked me to come to her side. "Oh no," I thought, "what does she want with me?" I walked over to them and noticed that the woman who had testified of her spinal healing was also afflicted by a goiter or tumor under her chin. As I watched intently, Kathryn touched the woman's neck, the goiter moved, then disappeared completely! Then my knees buckled under me and I felt like I was floating. I was filled with a sense of deep peace and joy. The next thing I knew, I was being helped to my feet. I had been "slain in the Spirit." I didn't want it to happen but it did. This dignified priest who didn't want to make a spectacle of himself was slain in the Spirit five more times in that same afternoon. So much for my dignity.

This phenomenon did not happen to me again until I went to the Third World Conference on the Holy Spirit in Jerusalem in 1976. I visited the Church of the Holy Sepulchre and was led to a cave beneath the main altar that is believed to be the site of Jesus' burial. There, a Coptic priest asked if I wanted his blessing. I agreed. He sprinkled me with sanctified water, laid his hand on my head and then, just as had happened at the

143

Kathryn Kuhlman service, I was overcome by the Spirit.

The next evening the Reverend Trevor Dearing ministered at the conference. After his presentation he began to lay hands on those who presented themselves for ministry. Almost all who came forward were slain in the Spirit. He asked me to help him minister, which I did. The first person I laid my hands on was immediately slain in the Spirit. This had never happened to me before, so I was taken aback. I closed my eyes, thanked the Lord for this confirmation of my ministry and just continued to lay my hands on the people who came before me. And it happened again and again until more than a hundred people were slain in the Spirit—through me.

Since that time, slaying in the Spirit has accompanied my ministry and I thank Jesus for it.

Those who want to study this phenomenon—either for further information or because they have doubts about the theological biblical authenticity of it—would be well rewarded by reading George Maloney's article about it in the November 1, 1976 issue of *Crux*. Maloney is a Jesuit priest and addresses his subject with thoroughness and objectivity.

Correspondence with the author may be directed to the following address:

Father Joseph Orsini
c/o Logos
201 Church Street
Plainfield, N.J. 07060